Historical American Biographies

JOHN WESLEY POWELL

Explorer of the Grand Canyon

Roger A. Bruns

Enslow Publishers, Inc.

44 Fadem Road	PO Box 38
Box 699	Aldershot
Springfield, NJ 07081	Hants GU12 6BP
USA	UK

Library of Congress Cataloging-in-Publication Data

Bruns, Roger.
    John Wesley Powell : explorer of the Grand Canyon / Roger A. Bruns.
        p. cm. — (Historical American biographies)
    Includes bibliographical references (p.) and index.
    Summary: A biography of the geologist who first explored the Colorado
River and the Grand Canyon.
    ISBN 0-89490-783-2
    1. Powell, John Wesley, 1834–1902—Juvenile literature. 2. Explorers—
United States—Biography—Juvenile literature. 3. Colorado River
(Colo.-Mexico)—Discovery and exploration—Juvenile literature. 4. Grand
Canyon (Ariz.)—Discovery and exploration —Juvenile literature. 5. West
(U.S.)—Discovery and exploration—Juvenile literature. [1. Powell, John
Wesley, 1834-1902. 2. Explorers. 3. Colorado River (Colo.-Mexico)—
Discovery and exploration. 4. Grand Canyon (Ariz.)—Discovery and
exploration. 5. West (U.S.)—Discovery and exploration.]
    I. Title. II. Series.
    F788.P68B78 1997
    550'.92
    [B]—dc20   96-32600
                                                             CIP
                                                              AC

Printed in the United States of America

10 9 8 7 6 5 4 3 2 1

Photo Credits: National Archives, pp. 11, 17, 31, 41, 55, 63, 65, 67, 79,
84, 111; National Museum of Natural History, National Anthropological
Archives, Smithsonian Institution, pp. 4, 61, 74, 86, 88; Photograph by
E. O. Beauman, 1871, p. 60; Stephen Klimek, p. 48.

Cover Photo: Jane Birch, Reston, Virginia (background); National
Archives (inset).

CONTENTS

This painting shows Powell leading his men through the rapids.

1

INTO "THE GREAT UNKNOWN"

The bearded, one-armed adventurer led his men down the river into the giant canyon. The boats plunged, darting and thrashing between rocks and over perilous falls. This was John Wesley Powell's great challenge—to ride the Colorado River into the Grand Canyon, the spectacular western gorge that had never before been explored. It was a place he called "the Great Unknown."[1]

The canyon walls soared to incredible heights. The crashing water boomed, growing louder by the second. On both sides of the river, the granite walls, slick with water and mud, closed in. For a time, the men got out

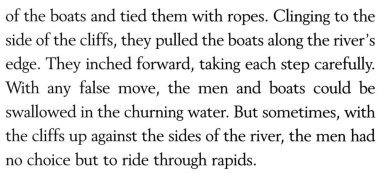

Navajo Legend and the Grand Canyon
The Navajo tell of a great flood that threatened their ancestors with drowning. The rushing waters formed a river that tore a giant gorge through the mountains. Into the raging river the Navajo jumped, turned themselves into fish, and escaped the flood. The great gorge, the legend says, is the Grand Canyon. Out of respect to their ancestors, some Navajo still do not eat fish.[2]

of the boats and tied them with ropes. Clinging to the side of the cliffs, they pulled the boats along the river's edge. They inched forward, taking each step carefully. With any false move, the men and boats could be swallowed in the churning water. But sometimes, with the cliffs up against the sides of the river, the men had no choice but to ride through rapids.

Suddenly, the boats hurtled forward and down, swirling and crashing in the white foam. Powell later remembered:

> We strike a glassy wave and ride to its top, down again into the trough, up again on a higher wave, and down and up on waves higher and still higher until we strike one just as it curls back, and a breaker rolls over our little boat. Still on we speed, shooting past projecting rocks, till the little boat is caught in a whirlpool and spun round several times. At last we pull out. . . .[3]

They had survived. But even greater dangers loomed ahead.

2

PRAIRIE DAYS: SONG OF THE OUTDOORS

John Wesley Powell was a child of immigrants. His father, Joseph Powell, was a Methodist preacher from England. He and his wife, Mary Dean Powell, settled in northern New York in the early 1830s. The Powells had a son, Fletcher, who died in infancy in 1832.[1] On March 24, 1834, Mary gave birth to John Wesley Powell, the family's second son. He was named after the great founder of the Methodist church, John Wesley.

The family called the boy Wes. Joseph Powell hoped Wes would be a preacher like he was. But Wes had other interests. The family home was in the lush region of the Genessee Mountains. Wes spent a lot of time wading along creeks, fishing, collecting rocks and Native American relics, and studying plants, insects, and animals.[2]

The family moved to a town in southern Ohio called Jackson. There, Wes walked through quarries, and talked to men who worked the salt mines and the iron furnaces. He also joined groups of hikers who explored the caves and rolling hills.

Wes's early education was often spotty and interrupted. But his keen and curious mind never rested. He later gained a good education in preparatory schools and colleges in several states.

In his very early years, he was taught reading and other subjects by his family, and especially by a family friend in Ohio named George Crookham. Crookham had a private museum of Native American relics and specimens of rocks and insects, as well as a small library of scientific works. By the time he was a teenager, Wes, encouraged by Crookham, was reading a wide variety of books, especially on nature—books on shells, snakes, and relics.[3]

In 1845, Joseph and Mary Powell took their family further west to Wisconsin, near the Illinois border. They purchased a parcel of land near Sharon, Wisconsin. Here, the growing family could maintain a small farm while Joseph continued his preaching. Mary Powell had given birth to seven more children in Ohio: five girls—Martha, Mary, Lida, Nell, and Juliet; and two boys—Walter and Bram.[4]

Although barely twelve years of age, Wes, the oldest child of a growing family, was given the responsibility of managing the farming activities. The boy learned in these years what it meant to turn land that had been previously untouched by the plow into valuable farm fields. He chopped down trees, uprooted shrubs, plowed the cleared ground, and planted. For Wes and his brothers and sisters, the work was difficult and exhausting.[5]

In May 1847, a large band of the Winnebago tribe camped near the Powell homestead. Wes visited the camp several times and learned about their clothing and their dances. He listened to stories told to him by those who could speak English. Wes began to collect Native American ornaments and tools that local farmers had dug up. He was introduced to a mysterious new world.[6]

Wes also made long trips alone in his boat on the Mississippi and Ohio rivers. Powell yearned to wander. He had a craving to see more, to learn more, especially in the outdoors. As a part of his large family, he felt trapped and unsatisfied. In October 1850, at the age of sixteen, Wes left home to live on his own and to attend school.[7]

Beginning a Life of Education

He moved to Janesville, Wisconsin, where he was hired as a part-time laborer on a local farm. He also began to attend classes in a one-room schoolhouse. Later, he attended the Illinois Institute, which his father had helped to organize. He did all of this on his own. His father refused to pay for Wes's education unless he studied to be a preacher. Wes refused.

After only two years, Wes Powell himself became a teacher. He took a job in Jefferson County, Wisconsin, as a schoolmaster. His salary was fourteen dollars a month. Some of the students of the eighteen-year-old Powell were as old as he.

Powell continued to read every book he could find on geology and Native Americans. He gave lectures in the local community on the things he had learned about other parts of the country. He spoke about explorers and Native American tribes and about ancient archaeology.

In 1855, Powell began to take science classes at the Illinois College at Jacksonville. During that summer, he purchased a small boat, traveled the Mississippi River, and spent four months gathering plants and fossil specimens in Wisconsin. It was the first of many expeditions he would take down the Mississippi.

Also in 1855, Powell met Emma Dean. She was the daughter of Mrs. Powell's brother, Joseph Dean. John Wesley Powell and Emma Dean were cousins. She was beautiful and energetic. She eagerly listened to Powell's plans for traveling and discovering. Emma wanted to become part of those plans. The parents of Wes and Emma discouraged them from marriage because of their family relationship. But the two became engaged.[8]

In 1858, Powell entered Oberlin College in Ohio, where he studied Greek and Latin and learned about botany, the science of plants. Later, he moved to Illinois, and joined a natural history society that was beginning a project to identify the plants, animals, and minerals in the state. His own collection of fossils, shells, plants, reptiles, and minerals grew large. So did his desire to explore new parts of the country. With each new spring, Powell was again on the move. And each new adventure was more ambitious—trips to Pittsburgh, Pennsylvania, to the Iron Mountain region of Missouri, and to Canada.

The young and scholarly Wes Powell became a well-known figure in Illinois among those interested in

Emma Dean Powell

The Naturalists

The Americans who began moving into the vast areas west of the Mississippi River included explorers, trappers, soldiers, traders, missionaries, and settlers. But the West was relatively unknown in terms of its natural history (its plant and animal life, its geography, and other features of the land). The job of identifying the natural history fell to a group of professionals known as "naturalists." They included individuals skilled in the study of various subjects including: botany (plants), ornithology (birds), mammalogy (mammals), ethnology (races and cultures of mankind), paleontology (fossils), geology (rocks and physical changes of the land), and meteorology (weather and climate).

natural history and science. Intelligent and energetic, with his driving need to discover, he was marking out a life as a teacher and scientist.[9]

But in the spring of 1861, Wes Powell's life, along with the lives of millions of other Americans, was suddenly and violently interrupted. On April 15, following the attack by Southern troops upon Fort Sumter, in South Carolina, President Abraham Lincoln called for troops to defend the Union. The Civil War had begun. John Wesley Powell became one of thousands of young Americans who answered the call. He volunteered for the Union Army.[10]

A QUALITY OF LEADERSHIP

On May 8, 1861, Wes Powell and a small number of others assembled at the courthouse in Hennepin, Illinois, to join the Army. They enlisted in the Twentieth Illinois Volunteer Infantry.

Wes and the others were soon in St. Louis, Missouri, the gathering point for a great Army that was preparing to invade the South. On October 8, 1861, under the command of General Ulysses S. Grant, Powell became a captain of artillery. His job was to supervise the construction of fortifications to protect Army troops.[1]

In mid-November, the young captain had a special request for General Grant. He asked to be allowed to go to Detroit, Michigan, to get married. Grant allowed him to make the trip. John Wesley Powell and Emma Dean exchanged marriage vows in a simple ceremony at the First Baptist Church, on November 28.

His wife would now accompany Powell on his adventures. When Powell rejoined his military unit a few days later, his bride was along as a nurse.[2]

Shiloh

At dawn on April 6, 1862, in a peach orchard in Tennessee, distant drum rolls and bugle calls awoke the Union troops in Battery F. Suddenly, the roar of artillery, the crackling fire of small arms, and the shouts and screams of men filled the air. The Tennessee countryside was plunged into chaos and confusion.

A young captain signaled his battery to mount and advance. The troops charged into the fighting, bayonets slashing and guns firing. Cannonballs ripped into the line of troops. Horses and men fell. The peach blossoms cut by bullets reminded some observers of falling snow.[3]

As Captain Powell raised his right arm to signal "fire," a bullet that had lost momentum glanced off his wrist and buried itself near his elbow. Gripped by pain, he sank to the ground, blood spurting from the wound. After a fellow soldier tied on a

Major General Grant on the Battle of Shiloh
Major General Ulysses S. Grant wrote to his wife, Julia Dent Grant, April 8, 1862, on the Battle of Shiloh:

"Dear Julia, Again another terrible battle has occurred in which our arms have been victorious. For the number engaged and the tenacity with which both parties held on for two days, during an incessant fire of musketry and artillery, it has no equal on this continent. . . . The loss on both sides was heavy probably not less than 20,000 killed and wounded altogether."[4]

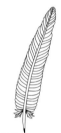

tourniquet to stop the flow of blood, another lifted the captain on a horse. As he headed for a Union hospital boat on the nearby Tennessee River, he saw thousands of dead and wounded men along the way. They were fellow casualties of the Battle of Shiloh.[5]

Captain Powell was taken to a hospital at a nearby town. His young bride was waiting for him. They had been married less than five months. The young soldier was told that the wound would not heal, that surgeons would have to cut off his arm.

On April 8, the operation was performed. For several days, doctors and friends and Emma waited for Powell's fever to subside. It did. Although he had lost an arm, Captain Powell had survived.

On June 30, less than two months after the Battle of Shiloh, Powell rejoined Battery F at Corinth, Tennessee. One by one the men greeted the wounded captain. Tears filled his eyes.[6]

Back to Battle

The loss of an arm did not end Powell's service to the Union Army. Although burdened by continuing pain, he nevertheless carried on. In May 1863, Powell was in Mississippi under the command of General Grant. Through mud and swamps, for more than three hundred miles, the wagons moved toward Vicksburg. When the troops reached an area north of the city, Powell was ordered to supervise the construction of two bridges across a stream. By the light of bonfires, the men worked through the night. By dawn, two full divisions of men marched across. The long fight for Vicksburg had begun.

For several weeks, Powell helped direct the building of trenches and earthworks at Vicksburg to protect Union troops from Confederate shelling. His men slowly dragged heavy armaments closer and closer to the Confederate lines. On the Fourth of July, a white flag of surrender appeared from behind enemy lines. At least on this day, at this place, no more young Americans would die in the Civil War.

John Wesley Powell

During the Vicksburg siege, Powell, faced with enormous stress and physical demands as well as an inadequate food supply, had lost weight and strength. The arm stump caused severe pain, as it would for the rest of his life. The stump would be too sensitive to bear an artificial limb.[7]

He went north to undergo a second operation. While recovering, he received notice of his promotion to chief of artillery with the rank of major.[8]

Again, Powell returned to the battle lines, reporting at Natchez, Mississippi. In the spring and summer of 1864, Major Powell was given the responsibility of organizing and training a regiment of African-American troops. As with all other assignments Powell had undertaken in the war, he performed this one magnificently.

Powell's service to the Union cause in the war ended in early 1865 with his honorable discharge. Courage, dedication, sacrifice, intelligence—the young officer had demonstrated all of these qualities. The loss of an arm, although physically and emotionally shattering, had not stopped him. The hardship and danger had not stopped him. Men with whom he had fought and worked relied on him and trusted him. He had, they all said, an extraordinary ability to inspire others. For Powell, the Civil War sparked within himself the drive, energy, and organizational ability to be a leader.[9]

But Powell was not, at heart, a military man. During the long siege at Vicksburg, there were many lulls in the fighting when he found time to study the hills and the steep ravines around the Mississippi River town. He found time to gather fossils, seashells, rocks, arrowheads, and minerals. He took notes on the geological formations. In the middle of the war, Powell had followed his deepest interest and passion—to explore and discover the mysteries and secrets of America's lands.[10]

4

To Uncover Nature's Secrets

John Wesley Powell emerged from the horror and tragedy of the Civil War physically handicapped but clear in purpose. In 1865, he began his first term as a professor of geology at Illinois Wesleyan University in Bloomington, Illinois. He taught botany and other natural sciences, including geology. He gave field trips. He also lectured to professional organizations and other groups throughout the state.

A year later, Powell became a teacher at Illinois State Normal University. At thirty-two years of age, with his shock of reddish brown hair brushed back, a beard usually out of control, and one sleeve of his coat empty, he was a memorable figure. Even though his voice was not overpowering, he dazzled audiences with his intellect and memory. He usually spoke with no prepared speech. He took his students on long field trips along streams and into woods to examine plants and collect rocks.[1]

Powell enjoyed his academic, influential life in Illinois. But within the young man burned the need for action, to be on the move, to discover.[2] He decided to lead an expedition, to explore untamed places in the United States.

The Lure of the West

Powell became increasingly fascinated by the Rocky Mountain area of the Southwest. In the middle of the nineteenth century, this large area was still nearly blank on United States maps because no one knew what was there. On many maps the large area was simply described as "Unexplored."[3]

Powell traveled to the West. He talked with Native Americans and hunters, read reports of other western surveys, and pored over the stories and legends. He visited the religious group called the Mormons, who had settled in Utah. They told Powell much of what they knew about the land adjacent to their own. He talked to other surveyors, mapmakers, and western explorers. He contacted fellow scientists. He checked books and published journals and articles. There was little recorded history.

Ancient Native American tribes had lived there. Explorers and religious missionaries attempting to spread the Christian gospel had reached certain parts of the area. Trappers told Powell of waterfalls, whirlpools, and caves. A Paiute warrior told him of trying to take a small boat through the rapids of the Colorado River and the violent sounds made by the crashing water. But the region was basically unknown.

With almost no money of his own, Powell would have to convince others that an expedition was worth the undertaking and that he was the man to pull it off. His ability to inspire enthusiasm for the proposed expedition was remarkable. In an astonishing performance before the Illinois state legislature, the confident Powell convinced the members to provide money for a natural history museum. Powell became the museum's curator. The museum, he explained, would feature materials gathered from an expedition to the uncharted areas of the American West.

The dashing Powell traveled to Washington in 1866, where his powers to persuade were just as impressive as they had been in Illinois. He persuaded General Grant, who was now secretary of war, to provide rations for the expedition as well as an escort of soldiers. From the Smithsonian Institution he got a loan of the scientific equipment he would need to conduct experiments on the expedition. He later convinced railroad companies to offer free transportation for his men. He persuaded other institutions and societies to provide money in return for some of the specimens he would bring back from the West.

In June 1867, Powell and eleven other scientists and naturalists and his wife, Emma, traveled west to the rugged mountain canyons and valleys southwest of Denver. There, they conducted preliminary investigations for the planned large-scale expedition. They collected fossils, minerals, reptiles, insects, and rocks. Powell sketched mountains and made geological observations.

In late July 1867, Powell made his first attempt at serious mountain climbing. The party prepared to take on Pike's Peak, one of the great challenges of the Rocky Mountains of Colorado. Up steep rocky slopes and into steep ravines, they slowly moved ahead. Fierce cold winds slashed at their faces as they passed the timberline and marched upward onto ground always covered by snow. When they reached the top, Powell and the others looked over a magnificent landscape of rock formations, streams, and plant life that spread out for hundreds of miles before their eyes. Emma Powell, wearing her green English felt hat, had become the first woman to climb Pike's Peak.[4]

For Powell this trip in the West was a period of learning and testing. It gave him valuable lessons in assembling a team of scientists and explorers, in handling scientific equipment under hazardous conditions, and in testing his own physical endurance without the arm he had lost in the war.

A year later Powell returned to the West, this time with funds given by the United States Congress. He led a party of mountaineers, scientists, and trappers into the Gore Mountains near Denver, and the upper canyons along the

Zebulon Pike and Pike's Peak

In 1806, a young United States Army lieutenant named Zebulon Montgomery Pike left St. Louis to explore areas of the Southwest. In what is present-day Colorado, he saw a towering mountain peak looming straight up from level plains. Pike decided to try to climb the peak, thinking that its summit was only a few miles away. Several days later and forty miles further on, Pike gave up and declared that "no human being could have ascended to its pinical [sic]."[5] Fourteen years later, three other explorers scaled the peak. Over forty years later, Emma Dean Powell joined her husband in scaling Pike's Peak.

Green River. During the expedition, Powell and his party moved through lands inhabited by supposedly hostile Native American tribes. He experienced no threats, no violence. He spent long evenings visiting the Ute tribe, learning their language and recording some of their myths and customs. Powell's vocabularies of Ute words were the first of that language ever written down. His collections of some of their crafts were of great interest to scientists at the Smithsonian Institution.[6]

The major was now ready for the great challenge. Southward lay the great unknown. There were stories about an enormous canyon carved by a great river that ran through the Rocky Mountains. The canyon was a wondrous creation of nature that did not exist anywhere else on earth. Powell could feel it within his grasp. He would attempt what no man had ever before attempted. He would ride that river between those towering rock walls. He would seek nature's secrets.

5

EXPLORING
THE
WILDERNESS

According to an ancient Native American legend, an old, wise chief deeply mourned the loss of his wife. A Native American god came to him and offered to take the chief to see his wife in the happier place where she had gone. The god then made a trail through the majestic mountains to the desert land of eternal joy where the chief enjoyed a reunion with his loved one. When the chief returned, the god made him promise to tell no one of his experience. Then the god filled the bottom of the gorge with an angry, raging river that would engulf any others who attempted to pass through the mountains. Any person who dared to take that river, legend said, would surely bring upon himself or herself the wrath of the god.[1]

In May 1869, Major John Wesley Powell took up the challenge. The river was the Colorado. The great gorge was the Grand Canyon. Here, Powell said, he might add to the great sum of human knowledge.[2]

The Grand Canyon

For over 4 billion years, the explosive forces of nature had carved a magnificent geological area in northern Arizona. Volcanic eruptions, floods, droughts, winds, and shifts of land had created a huge canyon over two hundred miles long with an average width of nine miles. The jagged walls of the canyon drop over six thousand feet to the Colorado River below. They display in their rocks a fossil record of the earth dating from the first living organisms.

From the time of the first sighting of the Grand Canyon by Spanish travelers in the mid-1540s, the massive wonders of the area remained relatively untouched. Native Americans had roamed through part of the canyon. Beginning in the 1820s, fur trappers searched for beaver pelts in the area. In 1857, an expedition by United States Army troops in the West surveyed small portions of the canyon

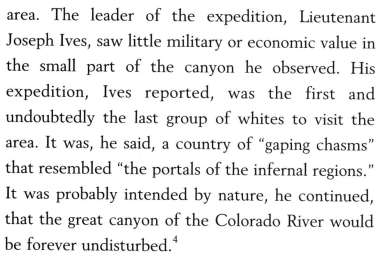

The Grand Canyon
LENGTH: Historically the canyon measured 217 miles along the Colorado River from the mouth of the Little Colorado River to the Grand Wash Cliffs. Today, the entire distance from Lees Ferry to the Grand Wash Cliffs is called the Grand Canyon. Its distance is approximately 280 miles.
WIDTH: Ranges from 4 to 18 miles, with an average width of 9 miles
DEPTH: Average, one vertical mile[3]

area. The leader of the expedition, Lieutenant Joseph Ives, saw little military or economic value in the small part of the canyon he observed. His expedition, Ives reported, was the first and undoubtedly the last group of whites to visit the area. It was, he said, a country of "gaping chasms" that resembled "the portals of the infernal regions." It was probably intended by nature, he continued, that the great canyon of the Colorado River would be forever undisturbed.[4]

But Dr. John Strong Newberry, a geologist on the expedition, saw the canyon differently. In his own reports, he talked about the geological formations, the ancient rocks, and the ageless river endlessly carving new beauty. He wondered about the sights that lay within the canyon walls.[5]

No one talked about challenging the river itself. No one discussed shooting the rapids—taking on the perilous, jagged passages and those twisting turns and white-water drops that could submerge a boat in an instant. Some mountaineers told about the terrible whirlpools in the river that would literally swallow any boat that got close to them. But on May 24, 1869, Powell, the thirty-five-year-old professor of natural history and one-armed Civil War veteran, began his quest to see the magnificent canyon from its floor. He wanted to weave through its raging waters, to explore its dangers and beauty, and to tell fellow Americans what this region, this blank space on the map of the United States, was really like.

It had been over sixty years since Meriwether Lewis and William Clark had made their historic trip across the American continent. Powell was about to undertake a trip that would reveal much about the last unexplored portion of the United States.

Powell knew that within the walls of the canyon was an invaluable store of information about the earth's natural development. Studying the canyon would reveal secrets of the earth. It would, he thought, be a kind of geological Bible.[6]

On the River

Powell and his nine fellow adventurers—hunters, Indian fighters, and guides—set out from Green River Station in Wyoming Territory to begin the journey south. The major had with him his brother Walter, who was emotionally devastated from months spent in a Confederate prison camp. The men called him "Old Shady," from a Civil War song. There was also Jack Sumner, a rough hunter and trader who had served as Powell's guide in the Rockies the summer before. Sumner had recruited four other trappers—Billy Hawkins, Bill Dunn, Oramel Howland, and Oramel's younger brother Seneca Howland. Three more men joined the party in Wyoming—a young Englishman named Frank Goodman, a high-spirited young adventurer named Andy Hall, and George Y. Bradley, a former Indian fighter from Fort Bridger, Wyoming.[7]

The team used Green River Station as its launch site because it was a convenient stop on the Union Pacific Railroad. Here, supplies for the expedition could be easily delivered.

The expedition was very much a personal undertaking, paid for by some small donations from institutions and organizations to which Powell had close ties. The Illinois Natural History Society and Illinois Industrial University gave money to Powell for the expedition. The United States government authorized the team to draw rations from army posts, and the Smithsonian Institution provided scientific instruments.[8]

Powell designed the boats himself. There were three twenty-one-foot crafts of white oak and a smaller sixteen-foot boat of pine better suited to maneuver through the narrow parts of the twisting river. The smaller boat was named *Emma Dean*, after Powell's wife. The others were called the *Kitty Clyde's Sister*, the *No Name*, and the *Maid of the Canyon*.

Green River Station, Wyoming Territory, was the spot Powell chose to launch his expeditions to the Grand Canyon.

With Major Powell in the lead boat, the *Emma Dean*, and with a crowd of onlookers cheering them on, the expedition left on the Green River. The boats headed south toward the Colorado River and the Grand Canyon. The journey would take them from southwest Wyoming, briefly through northwest Colorado, through Utah, and into Arizona. Powell believed the journey would last about ten months.

Within a few days, they reached the Uinta Mountains in Utah. There, a group of brilliant red cliffs led into the mountain range and into the opening of the first canyon on the journey. During the first part of the expedition, the river flowed swiftly. The waters, however, were not treacherous. This was a time for Powell and his men to learn how each of the boats handled and to test their own skills. Gliding through the increasingly rough waters, the four boats darted past red sandstone cliffs. Brilliant, shimmering colors of green, gray, and brown danced off the waves. They rode in relatively calm water, but the journey ahead would become increasingly perilous. The mountains looming ahead must have reminded Powell of the old Indian legend. But he forged ahead.

On June 8, 1869, they reached a canyon surrounded by massive black walls of rock. Leaping and then plunging, the boats skirted huge boulders in the river. The lives of the oarsmen now depended on their navigational skills. Powell would ride ahead, frequently moving to shore. He would examine the river and plot the course through the churning water.

Even with Powell's careful navigational planning, the river held some dangerous surprises. In a dizzying fall of over thirty feet, one of the boats, the *No Name*, was sucked up in foaming whirlpool torrents. The boat struck one of the great river boulders and some of the cargo splashed into the water. Powell later wrote about the struggles of the men through those terrifying few minutes: "Still they clung to her sides and clambered in again and saved part of the oars," Powell said, but "they went, two or three hundred yards to another rocky rapid just as bad, and the boat struck again . . . and was dashed to pieces. The men were thrown into the river and carried beyond my sight."[9] The men grabbed floating pieces of wood and hung on as they darted through the rampaging water. Frank Goodman, who had swallowed a lot of water, clung weakly to a boulder along the side of the river. They pulled him out barely before he drowned.

Although the *No Name* was destroyed, all of the men survived. Powell said that he felt as if they "had been on a voyage around the world and wrecked on a distant coast." Powell called the place "Disaster

Falls."[10] They had lost nearly a third of their food and some of the scientific instruments in the raging water. They had not yet even reached the Colorado River.

A Near Tragedy

On the morning of June 18, Powell set out with Bradley to climb a thousand-foot-high rocky cliff. They were trying to get a view of the direction of the river and the severity of the foaming white water. As the two Civil War veterans inched along slick crevices in the wall, Powell became trapped between the rocks. With a possible fall of eighty feet facing him and with only one arm to hang on, Powell clung to the side of the sandstone cliff trying to remain motionless.

Later, he remembered the ordeal: "I find I can get up no farther and cannot step back, for I dare not let go with my hand and cannot reach foothold below without. I call to Bradley for help." As Bradley scrambled to help his leader, Powell realized his predicament. "The moment is critical. Standing on my toes, my muscles begin to tremble. It is sixty or eighty feet to the foot of the precipice. If I lose my hold I shall fall to the bottom and then . . . tumble still farther down the cliff."[11]

Bradley maneuvered to a rock above, took off his pants, and held them down for Powell to grasp. The gritty leader released his hold of the rocks, quickly latched onto the pants, and, with Bradley's help, pulled himself to safety. Despite the close call, the two men continued their climb to the top. After finishing their scientific observations, they returned to camp.[12]

On July 8, the party now entered into what Powell later called "a region of the wildest desolation."[13] The river increased its pace, and the rapids spun the boats in crazy, unpredictable motions. Jutting rocks intruded on the path of the boats. The men lost some of their oars in the turbulence and were forced to stop and cut timber to make new ones. They were frequently tossed from the boats. They lost an increasing amount of supplies, blankets, and guns. "Another wave rolls our boat over," Powell wrote, "and I am thrown some distance into the water."[14]

The men also suffered from mosquito bites, which covered their bodies. The men camped for several days. They rested, made repairs to the boats, dried damp flour bags and other foodstuffs, and prepared for the rest of the journey. Bradley jotted down in his journal that the major had a tendency to choose uncomfortable campgrounds. "If I had a dog that would like where my bed is made tonight," Bradley wrote, "I would kill him and burn his collar and swear I never owned him."[15] But the most difficult part of the journey still lay ahead.

When the expedition approached another canyon, one of the men, Frank Goodman, decided to leave. The young man who had joined the party because he wanted adventure, decided to get out with his life. This trip had been more "adventure" than he had planned.

On July 21, 1869, the party reached the Colorado River in southwestern Utah. Moving along in single file, the boats twisted through crashing water even rougher than what they had encountered earlier. Time and time again, Powell and the others were swept into the thrashing water. Their oars flew about. The overturned boats rocketed ahead. When they stopped along the river's banks, the men talked about the possibility of facing falls so steep that no boat, no experienced navigator, could successfully survive. They were in completely uncharted territory. No one knew how severely one of those whirlpools could whip a boat. What was the steepest drop in the river's path? No one knew.

Cautiously, slowly, they moved forward in single file. Their voices were drowned out by the roar of the water. On August 13, Powell and his men camped at the mouth of the Little Colorado River. They were ready to begin the part of the journey that held such mystery. They were about to enter what Powell called the "Great Unknown." Ahead of them now was the Grand Canyon.[16]

6

INTO THE GREAT GORGE

"We are now ready to start on our way down the Great Unknown," Powell wrote on August 13, 1869. "We have an unknown distance yet to run, an unknown river to explore. What falls there are, we know not; what rocks beset the channel, we know not; what walls rise over the river, we know not."[1]

The canyon walls towered above them more than two thousand feet. Large shadows played on the waters ahead. The scene was magnificent. In the quiet evenings after battling the river, Powell took notes about the wonders he saw in the Grand

Canyon. Along the banks, he saw ancient dwellings in the cliffs where Indians had lived generations before. He found a cliffside kiva, a sacred underground room that ancient Native Americans used for religious services. Later, he found other ruins, fragments of pottery, and writings on cave walls. These were the ruins left by a people who inhabited the area thousands of years before modern Native Americans.

Powell and his men saw grand arches, carved rock formations, and huge limestone mounds. He saw marble walls, polished smooth by thousands of years of wind and water. He saw brilliant pools of water. The journey into the mountains, he later wrote, was an experience beyond anything he had ever imagined. The richness of the land, the majesty of this spectacle of nature, was overwhelming.[2]

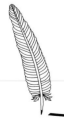

Cliff Dwellings

A cliff dwelling is a house or group of houses built by ancient Native American tribes in mountain cliffs and cavernlike openings. The dwellings were easy to defend because they could be approached only up the steep slopes from below. Powell saw many of these ancient dwellings in his trips down the Colorado River.

Powell was, the men had realized early in the journey, a different sort of man. He led them in singing lusty songs and then he quoted Shakespeare. As they talked of adventure and of someday becoming prospectors and finding gold, Powell took scientific notes.

Because of his physical limitations, Powell did not have to perform the same degree of physical exertion undertaken by his men. Nevertheless, even for Powell, the trip was a rigorous ordeal. As they drove deeper into the canyon, Powell himself must have realized that their fate was very uncertain. What he did not know was that newspapers across the country were speculating that the team had already perished.

The Challenge of the River

The sheer three-thousand-foot walls towered above them on either side. Here was a thin gorge, black and narrow at the base, red and flaring above. The great roar of the water grew increasingly loud. As they cautiously neared the sound, they found themselves above enormous craggy falls. Ledges jutted in their path. Rocks barely showed themselves above the water's surface. Water sprayed so intensely that the men could see only a few yards ahead. They saw the thrashing tops of so-called "rooster tails," where the water exploded against the unseen rocks below.

The party decided to camp and explore the area. Wearing rotting ponchos, the men slept in a driving rainstorm. They wedged themselves into some crevices that barely protected them. There were now only half the number of blankets needed. Food supplies were running dangerously low. The men were losing weight and strength. Bradley wrote in his diary, "If Major does not do something soon I fear the consequences."[3] Some of the men were considering whether to go further. Perhaps the Native American legends did correctly foretell doom.

On August 15, 1869, the men found some relief from the pounding river. "Early in the afternoon," Powell wrote, "we discover a stream entering from the north—a clear, beautiful creek, coming down through a gorgeous red canyon. We land and camp on a sand beach above its mouth, under a great, overspreading tree with willow-shaped leaves."[4] There the men found timber for oars and trout to ease their terrible hunger. Weary but satisfied as they had not been for weeks, the men bathed and stretched out to sleep on the sand. Powell named the stream "The Bright Angel."[5]

By mid-August, the party had only a few days worth of moldy flour and a few dried apples left on the boats. They were nearing the end of the journey, although they did not fully realize at the time just how close they now were to open land. For three months they had battled the elements and their own wills. They still did not know whether the most dangerous falls were behind them or ahead.

On August 19, they encountered whirlpools that spun the boats about as if they were toys. Men, oars, and equipment flew about in the churning white foam. Powell wrote in his diary that they were still "in our granite prison."[6]

But then, for a few days, the river leveled, the canyon widened, and the boats rolled along swiftly.

Powell's men look down at the Colorado River winding through the Grand Canyon.

On August 27, it all changed again. Bradley recorded in his diary the disheartening fact: they had reached "the worst rapid yet seen."[7]

It was an awesome spectacle before them. "The water dashes against the left bank and then is thrown furiously back against the right," Bradley wrote. "The billows are huge and I fear our boats could not ride them if we could keep them off the rocks."[8]

Powell discussed the situation with the men. All night long he paced around the camp trying to decide what to do. He believed the men had nearly reached the end of the canyon. Nevertheless, the rations and water were almost gone. Even if they managed to get through the falls immediately ahead without killing themselves, how much further did they still have to go? He and the others were not sure whether climbing out of the canyon would be any safer than continuing on the river. If they did climb out, what if they ran into a large area of desert? They would die of thirst. Powell decided they should go on, that they should run the falls and take their chances of clearing the canyon on the river.

Separation

Three of the men, however, decided to leave the party—Oramel Howland, his brother Seneca

Howland, and Bill Dunn. They chose to climb out of the canyon and to go overland toward an area where they expected Mormon settlements to be, about seventy-five miles to the north.

Powell gave the men two rifles, a shotgun, and a share of the pitiful rations still remaining. The major wrote a letter to his wife, Emma, for the men to deliver on their return. Sumner, one of the men who had decided to continue down the river, gave the three his watch to give to his sister in case he was never heard from again. The three solemnly packed up a few provisions, some guns and ammunition, and wished the others well. Bradley wrote, "They left us with good feelings though we deeply regret their loss for they are as fine fellows as I ever had the good fortune to meet."[9] Powell and others later called the falls ahead "Separation Rapid," to mark the place where the men parted.[10]

Each of the groups thought that the other was about to take the more hazardous trip. The three who left the expedition never reached their destination. Stories soon circulated that they had been killed by Native Americans. No trace of their remains was ever found. Powell later learned that the men had been killed by Shivwits tribesmen who mistook them for miners who molested one of the Shivwit women.[11]

With the departure of the men, Powell and the others prepared for the most severe challenge of the entire journey. Not only were they critically low on provisions and unsure of the exact distance still to travel in the canyon, the men were extremely weary. The intense, driven Powell tried to raise their spirits. They were on a mission of discovery, he said, one for which the team would be forever remembered. "But for years," he wrote, "I have been contemplating this trip. To leave the exploration unfinished, to say that there is a part of the canyon which I cannot explore, having already nearly accomplished it, is more than I am willing to acknowledge, and I determine to go on."[12]

Powell's measurements and his own geographic sense told him that they had conquered most of the canyon. Against a crisp, star-flecked sky, the major again took measurements and figured they were only forty-five miles from clearing the canyon, perhaps ninety or one hundred miles along the winding river. That was, he figured, perhaps only four days. Only four days to reach food and safety.

He gathered the men and tried to convince them that the monstrous whirlpool ahead would be just another of the treacherous traps already conquered by the expedition. The end did not lie at the bottom of that swirling water. For three months they had survived the river's pounding, had fought mightily to overcome the overwhelming feeling of helplessness against the power of nature. Although physically weakened, they had gained valuable experience in running rapids. They could run this one, he said.

Powell decided to use only two of the remaining three boats to run the terrifying rapids facing them. Into the rollicking, twisting water the boats swirled, oars splintering on the rocks. The men hung on to the damaged boats. Bradley later wrote how the party "dashed . . . into the boiling tide with all the courage we could muster. We rowed with all our might until the billows became too large to do anything but hold on."[13]

The two boats disappeared for several seconds in the white froth. Then they reappeared, with the men still clinging to them. They had survived. That night they sat around the campfire swapping stories they would tell and retell to their families for years to come.

As it turned out, the treacherous falls they had just managed to navigate were not the last challenge. Six miles further along they ran into another falls. Bradley was almost lost in the rapids. Powell later remembered seeing Bradley swept into "the mad, white foam below."[14] The other men, said Powell, stood frozen, fearing their friend would not reappear. When Bradley suddenly emerged from the swirling water, he waved his hat in the air. Once again, the explorers had avoided tragedy.[15]

Journey's End

The river had delivered its last blow. On Sunday, August 29, 1869, the country opened up. Before them now was the parched, brown desert spotted by creosote and greasewood, the desert's hardy plants. The journey was over. They turned to look back at the majestic walls of the canyon. They had seen its secrets. That night Powell wrote in his diary: "The river rolls by us in silent majesty; the quiet of the camp is sweet; our joy is almost ecstasy."[16]

The next morning, the men jumped into the boats at sunrise. They rolled along the gentle river, enjoying the new smells and sights and anticipating food and shelter. That evening, they came to the mouth of the Río Virgen, a muddy stream along which the Mormons had built several settlements. In the stream, they saw a Mormon man, his two sons, and a Native American man fishing with a net. Powell and his men leaped out of the boats and ran to introduce themselves. No introductions were necessary. The Mormon leader, Brigham Young, had already told his followers that men from an expedition into the canyon, or more likely the wreckage of boats and bodies of the men, might soon be appearing from out of the canyon.[17]

That night, in a small Mormon settlement below the Grand Canyon in Nevada, Powell and his companions feasted on fish, squash, cheese, melons, and biscuits.[18] Ten men with four boats had set out almost one hundred days earlier from Green River, Wyoming. They had traveled a thousand miles. Two boats carrying six men made it—the Powell brothers, Bradley, Sumner, Hall, and Hawkins. Bradley said later that he sat down to write a letter to his mother but he was so "intoxicated with joy at getting through . . . I don't know what I wrote."[19]

Powell had succeeded. He tackled a treacherous river. He did it without sophisticated equipment, without maps, without modern gear, without benefit of modern white-water boating techniques. He succeeded when other seasoned adventurers had not even tried. Years later a reporter asked Powell to tell him the secret of his success in making it through the canyon. "I was lucky," he said.[20]

This exploration was Powell's greatest adventure. It was one of the most honored feats of exploration in American history. Mountains and creeks that no one knew existed now bore the names that Powell and his men had given them.

Powell was fortunate to come away from the expedition with his life. However, these tales of survival retold in American newspapers across the country, laid the foundation for Major Powell's later

This map shows the location of the Grand Canyon and Colorado River in relation to modern-day state borderlines.

explorations. He would return to the Rocky Mountains of the Southwest for more exploration and scientific discovery. From this subsequent research would come the first photographs of the Grand Canyon, the important geological research of the Grand Canyon region, and detailed maps. From that research would come Powell's vision of conserving the magnificent resources of the West, a vision he would share with the nation.

7

SURVEYING THE AMERICAN WEST

The major returned from the expedition a national hero. The name of John Wesley Powell was now connected to the names of Lewis and Clark, John C. Fremont, and Zebulon Pike, other famous American explorers. Powell's expedition also placed him in the center of a national effort to explore the American West.

The Early Surveys

By the time of Powell's expedition through the Grand Canyon in 1869, other major projects had been launched to map and survey portions of the West. The state legislature of California in 1860 hired Josiah Dwight Whitney, a graduate of Yale University who was also trained in Europe, to explore the state and report on its mineral resources. Whitney's survey party ventured from the highest peaks of the Sierra Mountains to the walls of Yosemite, from the blistering deserts where the temperatures reached 120 degrees to the interior of gold mines. The California survey became a model for other surveys to follow.

In 1867, two years before John Wesley Powell's expedition down the Colorado River, the United States War Department hired Clarence King, an

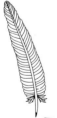

Mapmaking

The earliest maps of the lands west of the Mississippi River were done by the expeditions of Lewis and Clark, Zebulon Pike, and Stephen Long. By the time of Powell's trip down the Colorado River, the best general map of the West was the "Warren Map," named after its creator Lieutenant Gouverneur K. Warren of the United States Army. The "Warren Map" was based on the previous explorations of the West by the Army's Corps of Topographical Engineers as well as information obtained from trappers, traders, and other travelers. Powell's expeditions filled in the largest blank area of the "Warren Map"—the Grand Canyon.

adventuresome mountaineer and scientist, to explore and map a great one-hundred-mile strip across the West. The survey traced the route of the proposed railroad line that would cross the continent. The King team spent several years mapping the area, studying its rocks and minerals, and collecting plants and animals. King even chased down a few robbers, hunted grizzly bears, and scaled the highest mountain peaks.

The King survey provided the country with various kinds of information needed for the railroad project. His project introduced advanced scientific mapping techniques and uncovered important data on the mining industry. It also benefited from the services of T. H. O'Sullivan, one of the veteran battle photographers of the Civil War.[1]

The War Department sent another party into the western deserts in 1867. This one was headed by Lieutenant George Wheeler, a West Point graduate. Wheeler explored the deserts south of where the King expedition carried on its work, areas in which the United States Army wanted to establish supply routes for its forts. The team rode into the blistering sun of Death Valley and came out with a map. The King party also mapped other vast areas of the American Southwest.[2]

Ferdinand V. Hayden, who had explored the Dakota Badlands with several Army expeditions before the Civil War, was in charge of another major survey team. Hayden was appointed by the United States Congress in 1869 as the head of the "United States Geological Survey of the Territories." The Congress was anxious to discover information relating to coal and other valuable minerals in the West.

In his travels through the Rocky Mountains, Hayden uncovered substantial information relating to minerals. He also revealed the beauties that awaited other explorers, scientists, and tourists alike. Photographer William H. Jackson, who accompanied Hayden on his explorations, took the first photographs of the Yellowstone region and its geyser waters that pierced the earth's crust from deep below. Painters William H. Holmes and Thomas Moran captured on canvas the breathtaking sweep of the desert. Through these photographs and paintings, Americans could now get an idea of the natural beauty of the West. They now could see the fabulous rock formations carved by centuries of wind and rain, mountain peaks jutting thousands of miles into the clouds, and the magical colors of the land—the browns, yellows, and deep reds—playing off great shadows of light.

Hayden worked tirelessly to promote a bill in Congress to protect the Yellowstone region forever. On March 1, 1872, President Ulysses S. Grant

The First Photographers of the West

The nation's early explorers described the West in words, sketches, and paintings. Following the Civil War, Americans began to see from photographs the actual images. Photographers such as William Henry Jackson, Timothy O'Sullivan, and Jack Hillers endured the hardships and hazards of expeditions as well as the additional problems of their trade. The cameras were bulky. The photographers needed a variety of chemicals, glass negatives, tripods, and tents—gear weighing more than three hundred pounds. Often, they climbed up and down steep rock formations to take a single photograph. Their work opened the eyes of Americans to the wonders of the West.

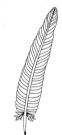

signed into law legislation that made Yellowstone the first of the great national parks. Hayden called the action "a noble deed."[3]

So John Wesley Powell in 1869 had joined these monumental efforts to map and record the geological and botanical features of the West. Powell traveled to many large American cities, telling the glorious story about his adventure down the river. He also revealed his ideas about how the mountains and canyons were formed. He explained that over the span of millions of years, the river had slowly cut through the layers of stone. He told how rain and wind had carved the jagged formations, and how new streams of water running away from the river had cut gorges and side canyons. The whole geological process, Powell believed, came from the slow effects of erosion from water, wind, and storms.

Planning a Second Expedition

Although the expedition had been an historic feat, Powell felt that he and the others had come out of the Grand Canyon with many things still not accomplished. Many of his notes and collections of specimens had been lost. Also, in the closing weeks of the journey, with their provisions running out, the men had been forced to abandon many planned scientific tests.

The major decided on a second trip down the Colorado River. He would repeat the journey, this time with better boats and with better equipment. He would now have a familiarity with the terrain and a better way to supply food. He would also have a longer period of time in which to undertake additional scientific examinations.

In the spring of 1870, Powell traveled to Washington, D.C., to meet with several members of the United States Congress. They included Representative James Garfield of Ohio, a strong supporter of federal aid for education and science,

This photo of members of the Hayden expedition was taken by William Henry Jackson in 1874.

and Representative Salmon P. Chase, also of Ohio, the chairman of the board of regents of the Smithsonian Institution. Through their vigorous support of Powell and his work, Congress voted to provide ten thousand dollars for additional explorations of the Grand Canyon region.

With its financial support, Congress made the Powell explorations part of those official government surveys already underway. The King and Wheeler surveys were under the jurisdiction of the War Department. The Hayden survey was sponsored by the Department of the Interior. Powell's survey, although originally placed under the Department of the Interior, later became the responsibility of the Smithsonian Institution.

Powell's second expedition, therefore, was not meant merely to duplicate the major's first expedition of navigating the Colorado River through the Grand Canyon; the second was to prepare maps and to take extensive geological observations and measurements on both sides of the river. It was to add to the work already being done by the other major surveys that were giving the nation an understanding of the geography and geology of parts of the American West now little known or understood.[4]

8

DOWN THE RIVER AGAIN

In preparing for the second expedition, Powell visited numerous Native American tribes in the West. Powell wanted to enlist the help of the tribes in locating water springs that he could use to supply the expedition. He also wanted to inform the tribes of the expedition itself so that no misunderstandings might arise.[1]

Powell was accompanied by the famous interpreter, Jacob Hamblin, a Mormon known for his extraordinary friendships with various Native American leaders. Hamblin believed that his principal mission in life was to cultivate peace between Native Americans and the white settlers beginning to fill up the West.[2]

Gaining Native American Help

With the legendary Hamblin at his side, Powell visited the Kaibab Paiute of Utah and their chief, Chuarruumpeak. The chief agreed to show Powell many of the water springs in the area. Powell also visited the Shivwit and Moqui tribes. He assured them that his expedition was not out to discover gold or silver. They were not out for conquest. His expedition was only out to learn about the land and its people.

Powell asked women of the tribes about domestic tasks. They showed him how they roasted seeds in wicker baskets over hot coals and how they rolled out meal on mealing stones. He asked young men about hunting. He engaged these shy people in discussions about language, customs, and even religion, a topic they usually avoided among strangers. He collected samples of their clothes, tools, and handicrafts.

For two months in the fall of 1870, Powell lived with these tribes. He learned much about their family life and agriculture, their ancient stories and myths. Powell moved comfortably among the Native Americans. At a time when the United States Army was waging war against tribes across the West, the tribes trusted and respected Powell. Over the course of several years he would become acquainted with the Ute in Colorado, the Hopi and Navajo in Arizona, and the Paiute in Arizona, Utah, and Nevada. He would learn to speak both Ute and Southern Paiute. "I can get along with the Indians by peaceable methods," he said.[3] Very few white men ever achieved the kind of friendship Powell established with various tribes. His relationship with those people would be a central part of his own life. The Ute and Shoshone tribes affectionately called Powell "Ka purats." The words meant "arm off."[4]

After Powell and Hamblin separated, the Mormon interpreter continued to talk to various tribes about Powell's second expedition and to gain their cooperation. Powell arranged for Hamblin to provide blankets and clothing to the tribes in return for that cooperation. Hamblin wrote to Powell in December 1870:

> We were visited by some of the Navajo Raiding Chiefs on our way home, they pledged themselves to do all they could to promote peace. I have not yet had any goods for the benefit of the Kaibab Indians. I would like to get a few for them if I could.

The superintendent of Indian affairs, Hamblin also reported, had provided goods for the tribes of southern Utah, "expecting they would be used in a way to favor your business next season."[5]

On the River Again

In May 1871, Powell was once again ready to take on the Colorado River. This was a new group of men. Although the major had loyal, courageous, and adventurous men on the first trip, this second expedition was not primarily for adventure but for scientific research. Of the men from the first trip, only Jack Sumner was asked to join the new expedition. Although he agreed to join Powell, he was unable to reach the Green River, Wyoming,

The men on Powell's second Grand Canyon expedition set up their first camp on the Green River, Wyoming Territory.

Powell (left) and his assistants pose for a photo on the second Grand Canyon expedition.

starting point by May 1 because of deep snows around his Rocky Mountain retreat.[6]

Powell was accompanied on this trip by his brother-in-law, Almon Thompson, an entomologist from Illinois. Thompson's two assistants, Walter Graves and F. M. Bishop, also joined the group. Graves was a cousin of Oramel and Seneca Howland, the men who perished at the hands of the Shivwits on the first expedition. Bishop was a Union Army veteran and recent college graduate. A third assistant, Steven Jones, was a school principal and Thompson's friend. The cook and handyman was Andy Hattan, an army acquaintance of Powell's.

E. O. Beaman of New York, a respected photographer, was part of the team at the beginning of the expedition but left early on. Beaman did not get along with most of the men from the beginning of the trip. A German immigrant named Jack Hillers was also a member of the party. Hillers would later take on the role of photographer.

Photographic equipment in 1871 was extremely bulky and heavy. But Powell decided that having a photographic record of the journey was worth the trouble and expense. Future generations would thank Powell for that decision. For the first time in history, the magnificent splendor of the Grand Canyon would be partly captured by the camera.

Jack Hillers took over as photographer on the second Powell expedition. He is at work at Aquarius Plateau, Utah Territory, in 1872.

An amateur geologist named J. F. Steward, with whom Powell had hunted fossils near Vicksburg, Mississippi, during the Civil War, was also with the group. So was seventeen-year-old Frederick Dellenbaugh, a young artist who was one of Powell's distant relatives. A young cousin, Walter Clement Powell, was also along, as was Frank Richardson, a family friend.

Thus, the second Powell expedition, much like the first, took on more of the look of a family hiking party than a scientific expedition. The group was eager, enthusiastic, and devoted to John Wesley Powell.[7]

Once again Powell directed that special handcrafted boats be built for the journey downriver. His own boat was equipped with a wooden armchair strapped to the middle. From this lookout perch, the major could better see the winding river ahead and signal the other boats behind in times of danger.

Powell's experiences in the first expedition proved invaluable in this trip as the team passed through the especially dangerous falls. Upon his extraordinary memory were engraved the sheer drops and fierce white-water traps that had nearly doomed his men two years before. Although the river itself gave the party plenty of trouble, some of the danger they encountered was of their own making. On one occasion, Frank Richardson accidentally sat on a hot coal while eating. When his pants ignited, he screamed "fire" and leaped into the river.

In late June 1871, the men found the remains of the *No Name*, the boat that had been smashed in one of the falls during the first expedition. To Powell, it was a dramatic reminder of the dangers they faced on the river.[8]

Powell gave most of the geographical work and much additional responsibility to his brother-in-law Almon Thompson. In Thompson, Powell felt great confidence and comradeship. His trust in Thompson allowed Powell to leave the party on several occasions. He traveled overland to take care of provisions and to visit his wife, Emma, who was staying in Salt Lake City, awaiting the arrival of their first child. In September, she gave birth to a daughter they named Mary. Powell first saw his daughter the following month.

The crusty Powell, with his bushy eyebrows, untamed hair and beard, and a cigar in his mouth, looked much more like a wilderness explorer than a schoolteacher or a scientist. Yet, he was all three. On the expedition he would suddenly sing very loudly some of the Methodist hymns of his youth or some Native American songs he had learned.

When the waters turned calm he would often reach for some books he had brought along and read aloud the poems of Sir Walter Scott, Lord Tennyson or Henry Wadsworth Longfellow. And there, along the river, with its

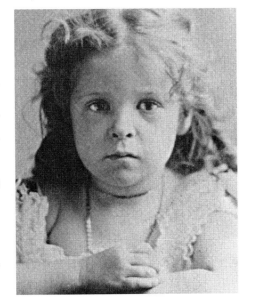

Mary, the daughter of John Wesley and Emma Powell, was born in 1871.

canyons and mountains and streams, the major wrote of the dramatic beauty of the "Buttes, towers, pinnacles, thousands and tens of thousands strange forms of rock, naked rock of many different colors . . . weird, strange, and grand . . ."[9]

Because of their ability to keep the second expedition better supplied than the first, the men were able to move along the river more slowly. They took careful measurements and observations and created new maps. As Powell had planned, the first expedition had been an exploring adventure; the second was a scientific survey. As winter approached, the expedition was still in southern Utah.

A Winter Break

The men made their winter headquarters at Kanab, Utah, a Mormon settlement that had been laid out the year before. The village was thriving, with an irrigation system designed to supply water to individual family farms. With a blacksmith, tinsmith, and other tradesmen available in the town, Kanab was an ideal location for the men of the expedition to wait out the winter snows and prepare for the rest of the trip the following spring.

For three of the men, the winter break became a permanent separation from the expedition. Bishop, the Union Civil War veteran who had been shot through the lung during the war, was physically exhausted. Steward, Powell's hometown friend and amateur geologist, had lost interest in the further challenges of the river. Beaman, the photographer, decided to strike out on his own, take more photographs of the Southwest, and head east to make money selling them.

However, one of the more disabled members of the team decided to continue. Steven Jones, the school principal, was suffering from rheumatism with its terrible joint pain and was often on crutches. But the gritty principal knew he was in the adventure of his life. When the team arrived at Kanab for the winter, both Steward and Jones had been brought in on stretchers.[10]

In late November, 1871, Powell brought his wife, Emma, their infant daughter, Mary, and the family dog, Fuzz, to the expedition campsite. For several days the expedition became a social affair

Powell's geological assistant, John Steward, left the expedition in 1871.

with dances, a few jugs of wine, singing, and great conversation. They were even visited by a few Native Americans.

On Christmas Day, the expedition had a party. For men who had been fighting the waters of the river since May, the spread before them was an amazing sight—ham, sardines, breads, plum pudding, and bottles of wine.

Through the winter months, Thompson continued drafting the maps using the survey measurements gathered by the expedition. The men worked on their scientific notes, diaries, and journals. They rested and ate well. Even with the improved supply system for the second expedition, the rations had been relatively meager. The winter break gave the men the chance to regain strength.

In the spring of 1872, the expedition made significant discoveries. Thompson located a river in Utah running into the Colorado from the north that the earlier expedition had not recorded. The men first named it Potato Creek. Later, the men changed the name to the Escalante, after the first white man known to have crossed through that area a hundred years earlier—a missionary named Father Silvestre Velez de Escalante. The Escalante was the last river added to the map of the continental United States.[11]

Northeast of the Escalante River was a mountain range that also had not been recorded earlier. The party named those mountains in honor of Powell's good friend and director of the Smithsonian Institution in Washington, Joseph Henry. The Henry Mountains of Utah was the last mountain range added to the map of the continental United States.[12]

Into the Grand Canyon Again

The second expedition moved down the Colorado and entered the Grand Canyon on August 24, 1872. For the first time, the miseries of this party seemed to rival the miseries suffered by the earlier team. As the boats took a ferocious pounding in the river, they began to leak badly. The men tried to tighten the seams, but they were not entirely successful.

On September 3, while Major Powell was standing up to get a better view of the rampaging water, his boat was struck by a giant wave. It lurched forward and turned over. Powell and three others fell into the rapids. All of the men survived. One of them joked with the Major about his efforts "in going to examine the geology at the bottom of the river."[13] Powell later wrote that he

> had an awe-inspiring ride. . . . The current set the boats against the broken waters along the foot of the cliff with great force so that she seemed to strike against a rock. But, passing that in a wild mad current through a narrow gorge that was frightful. On the river sped![14]

Frederick Dellenbaugh, the artist and historian who accompanied Powell on this second expedition and painted the first pictures of the Grand Canyon, wrote:

> The scenery assumed such gigantic proportions, the river ran with such fearful velocity, dropping in one sharp rapid after another in quick succession, that it was difficult to realize that we were still in the common world and had not slipped unawares . . . to some undiscovered and tenantless planet.[15]

With their boats crippled, and his men approaching complete exhaustion, Powell made a decision in September 1872 that he had refused to make in 1869. He decided not to continue through the rest of the Grand Canyon. He had preserved most of the notes for that part of the journey from the earlier expedition. Although he had hoped to take more thorough geological notes, there seemed to be no reason to expose the men to unnecessary dangers on this trip. After talking it over with the men, the major declared, "Well, boys, our voyage is done."[16] Thompson wrote in his diary about the reaction of the men: "All are very pleased. The fact is that each one is impressed with the impossibility of continuing down the river."[17]

Powell's second expedition down the Colorado, therefore, did not complete its planned journey. The second voyage had been primarily a scientific one, and Powell, in this situation, felt far less challenged

Powell's Words About the Grand Canyon

"The wonders of the Grand Canyon cannot be adequately represented in symbols of speech, nor by speech itself. The resources of the graphic art are taxed beyond their powers in attempting to portray its features. Language and illustration combined must fail. The elements that unite to make the Grand Canyon the most sublime spectacle in nature are multifarious and exceedingly diverse."[18]

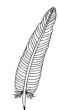

to conquer the water in the lower Grand Canyon. But the second expedition had accomplished far more than the first in securing valuable geological and mapmaking information. Powell made plans to continue his work.

As no other individual before him, Powell had revealed the mysteries of the Grand Canyon and other physical wonders of the West. Through his efforts and direction, the canyon had been studied, mapped, photographed, painted, explored, and measured. The "Great Unknown" was unknown no longer.

9

SMITHSONIAN PROPHET

In late 1872, Powell gave up his teaching position and purchased a home in Washington, D.C. There, at the Smithsonian Institution, he continued his work as director of the Geological and Geographical Survey of the Colorado of the West. In Washington, Powell was at the center of national power, at the center of scientific work in North America, where discoveries about the West were being debated and where policy about the West was being made. In Washington, Powell could make a difference in shaping the future of the West.

He and Emma moved into a house a few blocks from the Smithsonian Institution building on the

Washington Mall, near the White House. Their residence was a three-story brick home on M Street. A small courtyard in front was enclosed by a wrought-iron fence. Powell took long walks along the freshly built sidewalks with Emma and their daughter, Mary, to see Washington's statues and other sights. On occasion, they would visit the Smithsonian Building itself, where Powell had his small office, to look at the specimens of birds and Indian relics he and others had collected.[1]

The red-haired, whiskered, one-armed Powell became a familiar figure as he strode across Washington's Mall on his way to work, humming all the while. With its dark red sandstone towers reaching to the sky, the Smithsonian looked like a medieval castle. In his small office, the ex-Army major would entrance listeners with stories of the West. This was, after all, the man who had conquered the Grand Canyon, who had lived with Native Americans, and who had barely escaped death both in the Civil War and on the waters of the Colorado River. In his Smithsonian office, Powell wrote articles on natural science and met with legislators about water and land policy. He became the most visible man in Washington who knew about the land and the people over two thousand miles to the West.

The Smithsonian Institution as it looked in 1857.

Washington, D.C., was still a place that looked and felt unfinished. Years before, people called it a city of vast distances. It still was. Between the United States Capitol building perched on its hill and the White House several miles away, the city's broad dirt streets, often caked with mud, were being paved with wood and concrete. The city's first sewers were replacing open canals. Laborers were working on sidewalks made out of wood. But much

The Smithsonian Institution

The Smithsonian Institution was established in 1846 with funds given to the United States by James Smithson, an English scientist, after his death. The funds were given "for the increase and diffusion of knowledge."[2] Today, the Smithsonian has 16 museums and art galleries holding more than 140 million artifacts and specimens. Most of the museums are in Washington, D.C., including the National Museum of American History and the National Air and Space Museum. Two museums are in New York City—the Cooper-Hewitt, National Museum of Design and the National Museum of the American Indian.

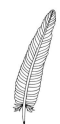

of the downtown area was still an open field. The Washington Monument, the magnificent structure that would one day point heavenward, was now only a third finished and looked like a giant stump.

A man of good humor and kindness, Powell made many new friends in Washington. He met Colonel C. E. Hooker, a congressman from Mississippi, who had lost his left arm in the battle of Vicksburg. Powell had lost his right arm. The two realized their hands were about the same size and joked about the waste of buying two pairs of gloves when one pair would be enough for both of them. They agreed that whenever either purchased a pair of gloves, he would send the one he could not use to the other.[3]

Powell's home was now Washington, D.C., but his laboratory was still the West. He would travel to Utah, Arizona, and Colorado to carry on the field work of his survey. Then he would return again to Washington to write about his findings, and to push for those policies he regarded as important for western development.

Discovering Nature's Secrets

As the survey work progressed, Powell became more intensely interested in how the Rocky Mountain region had been formed. He knew in his heart from the data he had collected in the two major expeditions and from his other work in the West, that the effects of erosion and other forces of nature had over the centuries carved the canyons and formed the mountain ranges. But his job now was to gather extensive data against which his theories and those of other scientists could be tested.

He assembled a team to explore the high plateaus of Utah, including Zion and Bryce Canyons and the Henry and Uinta Mountains. His own observations and the data brought to him by his teams in the field led Powell to strengthen his belief in the effects of erosion in creating the majestic landforms of the Rockies—the canyons, buttes, cliffs, and plateaus.

He became even more convinced in the power of water in shaping the forms, from the rivers cutting through mountain ranges to the storms smashing from above. It was as if an artist, through these tools of water, had sculpted the earth.[4]

In the summer of 1873, Powell met the artist Thomas Moran, who had done some work with the Hayden survey. The two established an immediate friendship and saw in each other the opportunity to advance their own work. Powell knew that Moran's exquisite paintings could help publicize the beauties and grandeur of the Grand Canyon and other areas of the Southwest. Moran knew that Powell could lead him to wondrous places and knew that Powell's reputation could enhance his own.

Early in August 1873, Moran stood at the rim of the Grand Canyon for the first time. He described that moment in a letter to his wife: It was "by far the most awfully grand and impressive scene that I have ever yet seen."[5] The spectacle of colors and shapes was, he thought, overpowering. To capture its exquisite beauty, the painter employed every combination of color on his palette, every sort of sweeping stroke, every delicate touch, every creative instinct he could bring to the work. Thomas Moran was, along with Powell, one of the first explorers to appreciate the primitive grandeur of the canyon and one of the first to share his vision with fellow Americans. His painting *The Chasm of the Colorado* was inspired by the violent thunderstorms that often sweep through the canyon's towering walls. It remains one of the great works of landscape art.[6]

In his geological observations, Major Powell was assisted by his good friend Grove Karl Gilbert, who during the 1870s became Powell's close fellow worker. Gilbert had worked for the Ohio State Geological Survey and for a time with Lieutenant Wheeler's surveys. When he joined Powell's group, Gilbert had more freedom and time to undertake his own geological observations and to reach his own theories on the formation of the earth's layers. His own research and conclusions were similar to those of Powell. The two men worked closely for many years in the field and in Washington, D.C.

Powell's other principal colleague in the field of geology was Clarence Dutton. A graduate of Yale, a Civil War veteran, a member of the Washington Philosophical Society, and a charming public speaker, Dutton joined the Powell survey in 1875. He worked for the survey for the next fifteen years.[7]

Powell had come to believe that his own survey and the other major surveys under Wheeler, Hayden, and King should be combined as one. In some cases the surveys were literally running into each other. They were examining some of the same lands. In addition, the leaders of the surveys were increasingly jealous of the work of the others. With all this needless duplication of effort and the petty bickering and political maneuvering, Powell began pushing hard for a more sensible, combined approach.[8]

In April 1874, after Hayden's party and Wheeler's men began working in the same part of Colorado, the War Department demanded an investigation. At hearings in Congress, Powell argued persuasively that the various surveys working

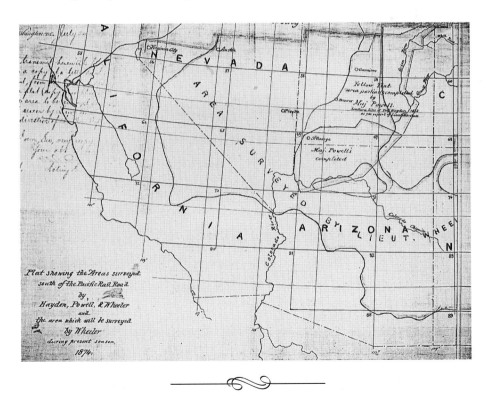

An 1874 map shows the areas explored by Powell, Hayden, and Wheeler, including the Green River, the Colorado River, and the Grand Canyon.

independently were costing the federal government a great deal more money than necessary. Although the Congress did not take action at this time, the case for a single survey had been forcefully made. Within a few years, the several surveys would, indeed, become one.

Powell was a busy man in Washington. In 1878, a number of friends gathered in Powell's home and organized the Cosmos Club, a place where intellectuals and scientists gathered to discuss the latest technological and political issues. The object was to advance its members in the fields of science, literature, and art. Powell was elected as its first president.

Powell also became president of the new Anthropological Society and a member of the Biological Society. Nearly a decade later, when the National Geographic Society launched its lecture series on expeditions and explorations, a series in which adventurers and nature pioneers revealed mysteries of land and culture uncovered in all parts of the world, Powell was the first speaker.

Powell would often take long buggy rides around the city with his good friend, the inventor Alexander Graham Bell. They would talk about the great discoveries and ideas of the age, from atomic theory to gravity. Washington was growing and so was the reputation of the fascinating Major Powell.

10

UNDERSTANDING THE NATIVE AMERICANS

Thousands of years before Europeans ever touched the shores of what is now the United States, native peoples farmed, hunted, created villages, and made pottery. By about A.D. 400, people called the Anasazi or "ancient ones" lived in the area where the present states of Arizona, New Mexico, Utah, and Colorado meet in the "four corners." They built circular pit houses lined with stone slabs and roofed with wood. They made cloth from turkey feathers and began to use the bow and arrow.

In the sixteenth century, Spanish explorers, venturing into the region, met the Pueblos and other tribes living in the Rio Grande Valley. The tribes lived in towns made up of buildings of stone and adobe with apartmentlike rooms. The buildings, each of several stories, had hundreds of rooms with ladders leading to the openings. The societies had religious leaders, civil organizations, and judicial systems.

Around the year 1600, Spanish colonists began a conquest of the entire area. It was the beginning of several hundred years of uninterrupted warfare between white men and the Native American cultures.

When President Thomas Jefferson gave instructions to Meriwether Lewis and William Clark at the beginning of their historic expedition across the country early in the nineteenth century, he emphasized the importance of gaining information about the tribes—their customs, living habits, and beliefs. Jefferson knew that such information would be valuable for the military in any conflicts that might arise in the future. It would also be valuable for the government in matters of land policy and in trading with the various Native American groups.

By the end of the Civil War, the military threats to the United States government by Native American tribes had diminished. In the years immediately following the war, military forces of the United States, with superior numbers and more sophisticated weapons, systematically defeated tribes across the West. From the Dakotas to Oregon to the Plains states to California, Native Americans were defeated in battle, slaughtered in raids, and moved to reservations, with little regard for their cultural or social conditions.

Southwest Tribes

In the Southwest, the conquest of the Navajo tribes was especially brutal. In January 1864, Colonel Kit Carson's troops trapped the Navajos in their Canyon de Chelly stronghold in northeastern Arizona. In the spring of 1864, Carson's American troops destroyed the Navajos' crops and seized their animals. Then they forced the Navajos on a three-hundred-mile walk to a reservation in eastern New Mexico. After a four-year imprisonment, the Native Americans were sent back to Arizona and confined on a reservation of mostly harsh and barren land.[1]

The tribes of Utah, Arizona, and Nevada encountered by Powell after the Civil War were mostly a desperate and poor people—Utes, Shoshones, Paiutes, and others. They had been driven from their favorite lands, where game and plants had been plentiful, into areas that made survival difficult. For example, the Utes, who had been herded into pathetic reservations after conflicts with Mormon settlers, were plagued in 1870 and 1871 by hordes of grasshoppers that destroyed their feeble attempts at agriculture.

Powell felt genuine sympathy for the plight of the various tribes. As a boy, he had dug up Native American tools and ornaments. In Wisconsin, he had watched the Winnebagos camp on his family's land. Before the battle at Shiloh, he had studied Native American gravesites.

E.O. Beaman, who broke off from Powell's second expedition, took this photo of a Ute warrior and boy at the Uintah Agency of northeastern Utah, in July 1871.

Powell knew that much of the culture of the various tribes was vanishing. He was working against time. In a few more decades, much of the Native American vocabulary, mythology, crafts, and handiwork would be lost to history.

Powell was confident that he had gained the trust of the tribes he had encountered. He told of hearing that a group of United States troops had killed some tribal members in Nevada. Native American delegations in Utah came to Powell asking whether he knew if the United States government had sent out a large expedition to kill off the tribes. "Some of them came three hundred miles," Powell wrote. They had learned "the utter hopelessness of contending against the Government of the United States" and were looking for the opportunity to progress.[2]

In his various trips in the West, Powell employed numerous Native Americans for his studies. "I have had from 2 to 20 or even 30 Indians employed, and I have had from 100 to 400 Indians encamped about me," he wrote, "and during that time I have no knowledge of their having stolen one cent from me."[3]

In 1872, George Ingalls, an agent for the Paiutes of southeastern Nevada, asked Powell for help in dealing with the tribe. At a great council meeting in October, the major addressed the Paiutes in their

Powell talks with a Paiute four years after leading the voyage down the Colorado River through the Grand Canyon.

native tongue, speaking about the advantages of adopting certain kinds of agricultural methods. The team also uncovered evidence of serious fraud involving United States federal agents in dealing with the Paiutes. Powell took the information to Washington.[4]

A Federal Commission

The following year, 1873, Powell and Ingalls were given a commission by the United States Department of the Interior to examine the conditions of the tribes of Colorado and Utah. The two arrived in Salt Lake City in early May, amid news of the clash between federal troops and the Modoc tribe. Despite the hostilities, Powell was able to visit several tribal communities. Later, outside Salt Lake City, Powell welcomed delegations of leaders from several tribes for discussions about how to settle the differences.

After several months of work, Powell and Ingalls made their report in Washington. They eloquently argued for an end to military measures against the tribes. They also argued for the Native Americans to be given land on which they could survive; land with proper soil, water, game, and timber. The report offered suggestions on how they could eventually join American society.

Reservations, the men argued, should not be prisons but places where homes, schools, and farms could develop. The people should not be given ready-made clothing by the government. Instead, they should be given fabric from which they could manufacture their own clothes. Each reservation should have a carpenter, blacksmith, saddle makers, and other skilled workers. A medical department should be organized on each reservation. Schools on the reservation should teach the English language so that the people could communicate effectively with white society.

The report also revealed an accurate sense of the racial difficulties encountered by the tribes: "the prejudices against savages which have grown through centuries of treacherous and bloody warfare, and the prejudices of race . . . are such that the Indian cannot secure justice. . . ."[5] Powell and Ingalls pleaded for greater understanding of these people, equal justice, and a forward-looking policy of education and training. "We may comfort ourselves," Powell wrote, "with the reflection that they are not destroyed, but are gradually absorbed, and become a part of more civilized communities."[6]

Powell wrote about the mythology of the Utes and others. They believed in many gods, he wrote.

The tribal council meets with Powell.

They believed that, many centuries ago, the earth had been populated by a race of beings of great powers. These were people who could supposedly make themselves invisible, could turn themselves into animals, and could bring others back to life. But even though they possessed all these wonderful qualities, they could not stop quarreling and fighting. Eventually, they turned into the various species of animals that we see on the earth today— birds, reptiles, fish, bears, wolves, rabbits, ducks, and others.

In addition to the animal gods, the sun and moon were also recognized by the Native Americans as gods, Powell wrote. The major also wrote about a Ute goddess called the "old woman of the sea." It was she who brought up the tribes of Utes from the ocean depths. It was she who gave them land and taught them skills.[7]

Powell did not condemn the efforts made by the government to transform the Native American population from "savagery" into modern civilization. The white missionaries and teachers who had roamed the West to educate Native Americans and to bring them to Christianity, Powell believed, were guided by noble motives. Much of what they had done had been beneficial. But they had expected too much. To believe that the Native Americans would give up the culture of generations of their

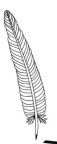

The Paiutes
The Paiutes were Native American people principally of the Rocky Mountain West. They subsisted by gathering desert plants and by hunting. They were skilled basket makers. Divided into two groups, northern and southern, they now live on many small reservations in Oregon and Nevada. It was the Paiutes, along with other Rocky Mountain tribes, among whom John Wesley Powell spent many weeks before his trips down the Colorado River.

people and take up new lives immediately had not been realistic. Nevertheless, Powell concluded that the efforts of religious organizations and the government had probably been "the wisest that human ingenuity can contrive."[8]

Powell believed that the Native American peoples should be slowly brought into white society. He did not think they should be forced to change immediately, but that they should be gradually taught and encouraged. Those Native American groups that had been torn apart through war and whose tribal organizations had been ripped apart had not adjusted at all to white society. When a Native American was cut off from well-established customs and laws and attempted to follow the life of a civilized man, Powell wrote, he often fell into despair, becoming homeless or even a criminal.

Let the Native Americans maintain their tribal organizations separate from white society, Powell said. Let them begin slowly to learn the English language and become educated in white customs and religion. Do not force United States citizenship upon them, he said. Instead, white civilization should be ready to give it to the Native Americans when they discover for themselves the benefits it offers.

Would the Native American population survive or would it become extinct? Powell believed that through education and enlightened government help, most Native Americans could, in time, become productive citizens. He knew, however, that the journey would be a long one.[9]

11

TO PRESERVE THE WESTERN LAND

Before the great explorations of the West, Americans knew little of the character of the land from the Midwestern prairies to the Pacific Ocean. The reports from the few explorers, traders, and travelers who had crossed various parts of the West gave little idea how much of that land was suitable for agriculture. There had been some talk but little reliable information about the "Great American Desert," a place of extreme heat and little water. Some of the stories about the desert led to great misconceptions and myths. Many people believed that if farmers began to plow the fields and plant crops, rainfall would miraculously increase. Somehow, people believed, "rain would follow the plow." Others even believed that the construction of railroads would mysteriously increase rainfall. Powell knew that such beliefs were nonsense.[1]

The Importance of Water

Following the Civil War, settlers in increasingly heavy numbers moved from the short-grass prairies of Nebraska, Kansas, Oklahoma, and Texas to the Sierra Nevada Mountains in California. Powell knew that their future depended on water. But it did not depend on water that would magically appear when crops were planted. It depended on the careful and intelligent use of the water available. It depended on irrigation projects, dams, and reservoirs to collect and distribute water.[2]

Even with effective irrigation projects, most lands of the West could not support the kind of farming carried on in the Midwest. If every drop of water from streams in the West were diverted to support agriculture, there would still be only enough water to successfully irrigate a fraction of the land.

As a teenager, Powell had run a small farm almost by himself. He knew the hours it took to create a ditch to drain water from a creek to a field. As a scientist, he knew the dangers of flash floods that could wash out a dam and bury crops. He knew

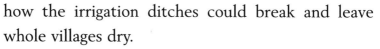

"The Rain Follows the Plough"
In the 1870s, many commercial land developers adopted this slogan to convince potential settlers that they had nothing to worry about from the Great American Desert. People who bought land in the arid West, the developers said, had merely to plant crops and rain would come. The entire idea had no foundation in science. It was a deception to persuade individuals to move west and take up farming.[3]

how the irrigation ditches could break and leave whole villages dry.

Powell strongly believed that the basis for western land policy should be on the amount of water available in the various regions. In a dry land, water was true wealth. Powell clearly saw that water was the key element for growth in the western United States. Manage and control it wisely, and the West could prosper; foolishly waste it, and disaster could result.

Three principal groups were competing for the lands in the West after the Civil War—cattle ranchers, farmers, and the mining industry. The cattle business grew so rapidly after the war that thousands of herds appeared in every state and territory from Texas to California. Powerful cattle owners ran herds over great areas of land. For them water holes and rivers became sources of survival and power. Large cattle companies began to control vast regions and, through that ownership, controlled much of the water supply.

At the same time, settlers began to fill parts of the West, all searching for farmland, all needing their own sources of water. As large water companies began to take control of those sources, increasing numbers of farmers struggled to make a living.

The mining companies were mostly in the mountainous regions of the West. Nevertheless, those companies also required water for extracting valuable minerals from the soil. For generations, these three groups—the cattle ranchers, the farmers, and the miners—would compete for western water. They purchased land where water existed and then sold the rights to use it. It was a struggle in which the future of the West and the survival of its natural resources were at stake.[4]

Powell's Report on Western Lands

In 1878, Powell produced a book on the complex land problems facing the American West. It was entitled *Report on the Lands of the Arid Regions of the United States*. A work based on extensive research, it outlined in startling clarity the needs for the areas of the United States that lacked sufficient water.

Through a broad program run by the federal government, he said, the areas must be surveyed for available water. Dams and canals must be built to divert water for irrigation. Reservoirs must be constructed to save the water. Land must be sold based on the kinds of use that the land itself could support. Lands with little water, for example, could be used for cattle and sheep; lands with adequate sources of water could be used for farming. If these steps were not taken, he said, "Many droughts will occur and many seasons in long series will be utter failures."[5]

Most of all, the *Report* emphasized that the use of western lands must be based on the cooperative use of water. The low level of rainfall required cooperative land and water management for the good of all. Powell suggested new laws to control the selling of public lands based on the amount of water in the areas and based on whether the land was to be used for farming or for grazing. This publication was Powell's challenge to the growing warfare in the West by competing groups who wished to control the water. In it was Powell's program to conserve natural resources in a responsible and scientific way. It was a program for which he would wage a vigorous battle.

Deeply worried about the rush to settle the West, Powell wrote articles in newspapers and magazines about the limits of water, about the dangers of spoiling the natural resources, and about the need to plan and control the growth of settlement. His views angered developers, ranchers, bankers, and others who believed that the vastness of the West did not need regulations to protect it. The West, they believed, did not need meddlers like Powell preaching against their interests.

Large land developers and cattle kings, men who were growing rich under relatively unrestricted land policies, accused Powell of trying to shut off the development of the West. They accused him of pushing the federal government into matters in which it had no authority. A member of the United States House of Representatives from Colorado called Powell a "revolutionist," involving himself in affairs "of which he has no proper conception."[6] A congressman from South Dakota called him a "tycoon of many tails" who knew as much about the arid lands as he did about the mountains on the moon.[7]

Powell warned early on about the problems of rapid development and the misuse of natural resources in an arid land. As a national spokesman for conservation and a pioneer in the development of government programs of preservation and geologic science, he remains one of the most important scientific figures of nineteenth-century America. His message is still powerful today.

In 1879, a year after the appearance of his *Report on the Arid Lands*, Congress finally created a single bureau combining all of the great government-sponsored surveys—those of Powell, King, Hayden, and Wheeler. The major had been waging an energetic political campaign for such a single bureau for several years. It was to be called the United States Geological Survey.

At the same time it created the Geological Survey, Congress approved, at Powell's request, the creation of the Bureau of Ethnology. In his work with Native Americans, Powell had devoted much of his energy to ethnology, the study of the historical development and characteristics of the races and cultures of mankind. Appropriately, the Bureau was placed under the control of the Smithsonian Institution. Here in the Smithsonian would be placed the records relating to the Native American as collected by Powell's survey of the Rocky Mountains. As the Bureau's first director, Major Powell would give national direction to the study of the Native American tribes.[8]

$\boxed{12}$

TWO NEW JOBS

By the time he became director of the Bureau of Ethnology in 1879, John Wesley Powell had for many years been accumulating data on Native Americans. He had studied their languages, customs, and religions. The new position enabled the major to expand his studies even further.

The Bureau of Ethnology

The new bureau studied the "science of man" as it was revealed in the lives of the Native Americans. It published materials on various subjects relating to the tribes—their habits and customs, architecture, history, family life, religious ceremonies, and languages. The Bureau controlled all of the materials on the Native American tribes of North America that Powell had collected in the Rocky Mountains. It also had extensive materials collected by the Smithsonian Institution from United States Army officers in the West, missionaries, Indian agents, and others who had made contact with various tribes.[1]

As the head of the Bureau, Powell assembled a team to bring some order and classification to information on the tribes. He wrote about the need to preserve what remained of the Native American cultures: "The field of research is speedily narrowing because of the rapid change in the Indian population now in progress; all habits, customs, and opinions are fading away; even languages are disappearing."[2]

Powell believed that perhaps all of this information, drawn together and made available to the public, would reduce the misunderstanding, fear, and ignorance regarding these people. Powell had barely settled into the job of Bureau director when he sent a team of researchers to New Mexico and Arizona to learn the customs and languages of the Pueblos and Blackfeet.[3]

Over the next few years, Powell and his team published books on tribal languages, medical practices, governments, myths, sign language, and picture writing. They classified the tribes into groups and identified over five hundred languages.

Warfare in the West

Wars between the United States Army and Native Americans were numerous and violent in the years after the Civil War. Between 1865 and 1890 the Army conducted approximately one hundred campaigns and at least one thousand smaller actions against various tribes across the West. Although many tribes scored victories, the force of numbers and technology overwhelmed the Native Americans. As each struggle ended, the government confined the tribes to reservations apart from white settlers.

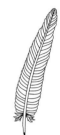

From Jack Hillers, the photographer who had accompanied Powell on his second expedition down the Colorado River, came hundreds of photographs. Hillers captured on film many tribes that were vanishing, including the Uinkarets and the Shivwits. The Shivwits had come into contact with only a few whites, even by the 1870s. They had meetings with Powell's friend Jacob Hamblin and a few other Mormons and had met with Powell himself. It was the Shivwits who had killed three members of Powell's first expedition, believing the men had attacked a Shivwits woman.

As Powell's Bureau assembled and published materials on the Native Americans, the major's own knowledge of the tribes became even more astonishing. In 1884, he attended a meeting in Montreal, Canada, of the British Association for the Advancement of Science. At the meeting, scientists displayed wampum belts. The word wampum comes from the Algonquin tribe of the East Coast of the United States. Wampum were bits of seashells strung into strands or belts and used, among other things, as money or for improving the memory.[4]

Upon seeing the display, Powell announced that a number of the belts were not made by Native Americans. He had seen wampum, he said, and this was not the real thing. The statement caused quite a stir. Some of the scientists at the meeting were very angry at Powell. Months later it was discovered that a wampum factory was operating along the Hackensack River in New Jersey. The belts at the exhibit had not been made by Native Americans.[5]

William Henry Holmes, Powell's successor as head of the Bureau of Ethnology, later paid tribute to Powell's work in establishing the Bureau and in making Americans across the country increasingly aware of the culture and history of Native Americans. Holmes declared that the major's work "will stand, not only for himself but for the nation, among the most important contributions to human history ever made by an individual, an institution, or a state."[6]

The United States Geological Survey

During the first years of Powell's service as head of the Bureau of Ethnology, Clarence King became the United States Geological Survey's first director. As the leader of one of the great surveys, King had attained exceptional knowledge and understanding of western lands. Powell had pushed for King's appointment. King later wrote to Powell in a letter expressing gratitude, "I am sure you will never regret your decision and for my part it will be one of my greatest pleasures to forward your scientific work and to advance your personal interest."[7]

Powell was happy at the Smithsonian as head of the Bureau of Ethnology. He was also pleased with the creation of the Geological Survey. The various surveys of the West, with their overlapping responsibilities and competing interests and personal antagonisms, had been merged into one agency. The Geological Survey, Powell hoped, could give much-needed direction to the nation in planning for the development of the West. Perhaps a single agency, given appropriate influence and power, could make an important positive impact.[8]

Clarence King was considered by many in Washington to be one of the nation's most informed and talented public servants. Charming, witty, a man of learning, taste, and social position, King had accomplished much in his own western surveys. His publication, *Systematic Geology*, written after the completion of most of his work in the West, gave him great standing in the scientific world. He was well respected in the cultural circles of the city. He seemed a logical choice to head the Geological Survey.

But King, as it turned out, did not last long as the head of the new agency. His health was failing. Also, he suddenly was seized by the opportunity to make an investment fortune in the mines of Mexico. With two wealthy partners, King formed a mining company and, shortly thereafter, resigned as head of the Geological Survey. He said that the best man to take his place was John Wesley Powell. President James Garfield, who had known Powell for many years, agreed.[9]

Heading the Geological Survey

In 1881, Powell became director of the Geological Survey. He would bring it to prominence and power. Unlike King, Powell was not interested in making a fortune. Unlike others in Washington, Powell could clearly see the many possibilities that this new government agency had before it. He knew it could help bring about the proper development of America's western lands.

Powell saw the Geological Survey as a great scientific fact-finding bureau. It would provide information and educate the nation. With both the

Bureau of Ethnology and the Geological Survey under his direction, Powell was in a strong position to shape public opinion and influence congressional action.

Powell was genuinely devoted to public service. He was a man who saw public service as one of life's greatest callings. In this new position, he could work for the interests of the country. He could fight against those who would exploit the western lands for their own personal gain. Powell strongly believed that government should undertake scientific research for the good of the country. He declared, "The harvest that comes from well-directed and thorough scientific research has no fleeting value, but abides through the years, as the greatest agency for the welfare of mankind."[10]

Under Powell's direction, the Geological Survey would explore the West to better understand how to use its national resources, irrigate its fields, and divide its lands for the good of all. The West would be studied with an eye on preserving its rich treasures.

As director of the Geological Survey, Powell selected reservoir sites, places in which to store water for later distribution. He selected canal sites. He was responsible for recommending to the president areas ready to be opened for settlement. Every settler who bought land in the West, Powell believed, should be assured that the land would have sufficient water.

Powell now wielded considerable power. This was a fact not lost on the development interests in the West. One angry Powell opponent called him a "Caesar."[11] A congressman from Colorado declared that the federal government should not intrude unnecessarily in the business of the people of the areas affected. "Do not shackle us with this folly," the congressman declared.[12]

But in 1886, nature made John Wesley Powell's observations about the West seem on the mark. For two years, the West was struck by a severe drought. Crops and cattle died, along with the dreams of farmers and ranchers. The writer Hamlin Garland said, "The sky, absolutely cloudless, began to scare us with its light."[13]

In a speech in North Dakota, Powell declared:

> Years will come of abundance and years will come of disaster, and between the two people will be prosperous and unprosperous, and the thing to do is look the question squarely in the face. . . . You hug to yourselves the delusion that the climate is changing. This question is 4,000 years old. Nothing that man can do will change the climate.[14]

In March 1888, Senator "Big Bill" Stewart of Nevada pushed legislation through Congress authorizing Powell to conduct a survey of possible dam sites. As Powell had suggested, something had to be done about the problems of controlling western water. Stewart most likely expected Powell to do a quick study, recommend obvious sites for dams, and then let the private developers go to work. But in this legislation Powell saw a chance to have greater influence than "Big Bill" had ever imagined.

Conflict over Western Lands

Powell launched a huge project to map lands across the West to determine how and where irrigation projects might be undertaken and where water reservoirs might be constructed. The sale of lands by the federal government, in the meantime, was to be suspended until the major completed his work. The project might, he believed, take six or seven years.

Powell saw the opportunity to change federal land policy. The current uncontrolled system of development, he believed, was rapidly destroying the future of the West. The government would have to bring about common sense and necessary order to save the western lands from further damage.

In magazine and newspaper articles, in speeches and letters, Powell explained his plan. The land needed to be carefully analyzed. The West needed irrigation projects and new dams on major rivers. The West also needed government-supervised land distribution to make the land more productive.

"Big Bill" Stewart was furious. He set out to take back from Powell the power that Congress, through his own sponsored legislation, had given him. Stewart held congressional hearings. He accused Powell of mismanaging funds and assuming unwarranted power. Powell was now a major target for Stewart and his friends. They were willing to try anything to oust the major from his position.

Powell fought back. When he testified before Congress, he reminded the politicians of his background—the loss of his arm for the Union, the trips down the mighty Colorado, his ability to deal with Native Americans without guns. He traveled around Washington giving speeches, holding meetings, trying his best to mobilize his own political force.

But even with his incredible energy and charm, even with the support of the many friends he had made in Washington over the years, Powell was now in the political fight of his life. Developers hated him. Big business hated him. Most western politicians hated him. No one, it seemed, wanted the government to go slowly on land sales. The West was a paradise waiting for farmers, developers, and other businessmen. Powell was standing in the way.[15]

Powell's enemies ignored the scientific evidence. They believed that most of the West, despite the lack of water, could be farmed or grazed. At one meeting of an irrigation group in Los Angeles, Powell declared, "I tell you gentlemen, you are piling up a heritage of conflict and litigation over water rights for there is not sufficient water to supply the land."[16] The crowd booed him.

This was one fight Powell could not win. In 1891, the Congress, led by Stewart and other western representatives, drastically cut the budget for the Geological Survey. They also cut off funds for the irrigation survey. Powell's power was gone.

With his views assaulted by angry congressmen from the western states and his funds from Congress drying up, Powell resigned as director of the Geological Survey in May 1894. Publicly, he said he was leaving because of his physical disability. The stump of his arm, on which he had surgery twice, was giving him continual pain. But he suffered more from the poor treatment given to him by the United States Congress.

Powell had been right about the matter of western water. As he had warned, thousands of western settlers later lost their possessions and even their lives to drought. He had given the nation an honest look at the needs of the western lands. He had developed a plan to fulfill those needs. But he had been defeated. However, it was not only Powell who had lost. The American West lost also.

13

THE FUTURE
OF THE WEST

John Wesley Powell will always be remembered
for his daring trips down the Colorado River
through the Grand Canyon. The image of this tough
Civil War veteran with one arm leading his men
through swirling white-water rapids will always be
an exciting part of the American story.

But there are other legacies of the life and work
of Powell. They are in the government agencies he
helped establish: the United States Geological
Survey and the Bureau of American Ethnology. They
are in his studies of Native American culture,
history, and language, which helped Americans

John Wesley Powell

understand the humanity and contributions of these people.

Perhaps Powell's greatest legacy was his vision of the future of the American West. In 1893, for example, Powell had declared that the issue of water would continue to plague the West. Time proved Powell correct. The battles over water have raged.

For over a century, this intense national debate over the role of the federal government in the use and conservation of the nation's western lands continued. Over the years new canals, dams, pipelines, and power plants began to harness the water to control floods, to irrigate, and to provide drinking water. But the questions have lingered. Even with advanced technological means, how much growth could the West tolerate? How should the decisions about growth be made? How could the nation provide the most adequate water supply to the West?[1]

As it became clear that unrestrained growth was jeopardizing timber and other natural resources, other voices joined a growing movement to conserve. President Theodore Roosevelt was a man whose greatest passion was exploring the wild places of nature. His views on conservation were much like those of Powell, and he admired Powell's work. In his speeches, President Roosevelt sounded very much like the major. Roosevelt warned of the dangers of wasting the natural bounties of the American West.[2]

Roosevelt's chief of the United States Forestry Service, Gifford Pinchot, the individual whom many have credited with first using the term "conservation" in referring to the environment, pushed forward a program that followed Powell's goals.[3]

In the summer of 1902, President Roosevelt asked Congress to create a new federal irrigation program. It would later become the Bureau of Reclamation and would pursue the conservation goals Powell had outlined in his grand plan for the American West. In his appeal for support for the Bureau of Reclamation, Roosevelt said, "If we could save the water running to waste, the western part of the country could sustain a population greater than even legendary Major Powell dreamed."[4] From the Sun River project in Montana to projects along the Rio Grande River, much western development relied on the surveys, scientific research, and mapmaking of Powell.[5]

In the 1930s, Representative Edward Taylor of Colorado, a man who had wanted to give control of western lands to the individual states rather than the federal government, changed his mind. Forty years after Powell's battles with the United States Congress, Representative Taylor saw waste and overuse and ugly competition over land and water.

He switched to Powell's side. He was now in favor of federal leadership in conserving western land, he said, "because the citizens were unable to cope with the situation under existing trends and circumstances. The job was too big . . . for even the states to handle. . . ."[6]

This debate over the role of the federal government in land issues continues to rage. Some argue that the federal government must have strict control of the public lands to preserve them and to provide for the best use of the areas. Others argue that the federal government should give up most of the control over public lands, that private companies and individuals have the fundamental right to buy and sell without federal interference. The lessons taught by John Wesley Powell are still there to be learned.

A farm boy from the Midwest with a patchwork early education had become not only a world-famous explorer but one of the foremost scientists in the United States. The boy who had wandered the creeks gathering rocks had become, through the sheer force of his intellect and energy, a man honored with degrees from great universities from Heidelberg to Harvard. In 1891, he was given the Cuvier Prize for his efforts with the Geological Survey. This prize is given every three years for "the most remarkable work either on the Animal

Kingdom or Geology."[7] He became a member of a dozen international scientific societies. One scientist later said that Powell knew more about Native Americans than any man alive.[8]

The historian Bernard DeVoto wrote in 1953 that Powell's *Report on the Lands of the Arid Regions* was "one of the most remarkable books ever written by an American."[9] The book, said DeVoto, was tragic in the sense that Powell's warnings about the possible waste of natural resources had been largely ignored. If his warnings had been heeded by his fellow Americans, said DeVoto, much lost land would have been saved.[10]

On September 23, 1902, at Haven, Maine, Powell passed away. He was sixty-eight years old. Until the final year of his life, the major remained actively engaged in research. Indeed, in the winter of 1900–1901, he made an expedition to Cuba and Jamaica to study the Arawak and Carib tribes.[11]

A Friend Remembers Powell
Fellow scientist and friend W. J. McGee said of Powell: "Things large to others were small to him. Things great to him were past the reach of most others."[12]

One can perhaps see best into the life of John Wesley Powell by looking at the American Southwest—the jutting lines of the mountain tops; the rugged vastness of its desert, dry but flowering; the character of its people, from the Hopi on the Arizona mesas to the Mormon towns of Utah. There is power and splendor in the lush canyons and buttes, on the rivers, and across the parched lands.

On one of his trips to Arizona, the major traveled with several others to examine some of the ancient pueblos in the mountains near Flagstaff. Among those in the party was his niece, Frances Dean Davis, an artist. One of the pueblo ruins was nearly inaccessible. But Powell and Frances Davis were determined. She wanted to paint the ruins. Powell and the other men climbed above the ruins and lowered the artist on a homemade scaffold. For nearly an hour, suspended on the scaffold, the artist sketched. Later, Powell was exuberant. "Make ready my steed," he said. "We are going out to see the sun set." Against the backdrop of magnificent colors, as the sun disappeared behind the Arizona mountains, the major burst into song.[13]

Powell spent his last summers at a cottage on the coast of Maine. It seems right that he was there, a place where nature's power reigns—the water, the big sky, the winds, the rocky coast. From the time he was a small boy, he had appreciated these things. As an adult, he taught the nation to respect them.

CHRONOLOGY

1834—Born in Mount Morris, New York.

1838—Family moves to Jackson, Ohio.

1846—Moves to South Grove, Wisconsin.

1851—Moves to Bonus Prairie, Illinois.

1854—Joins Illinois Society of Natural History.

1855—Becomes student at the Illinois College at Jacksonville.

1858—Selected as secretary of the Illinois Society of Natural History.

1861—Enlists as private in Union Army.

1862—Seriously injured at Battle of Shiloh, losing much of his right arm; Marries cousin, Emma Dean.

1865—Resigns with the rank of brevet lieutenant colonel; Begins college teaching career as professor of geology at Illinois Wesleyan University.

1866—Joins faculty at Illinois State Normal University.

1867—Leads a party of students to the Rocky Mountains under the sponsorship of the Illinois State Natural History Society.

1868—Leads another exploring party to the Rocky Mountains and spends winter on the White River in western Colorado.

1869—Leads major exploration down the Colorado River through the Grand Canyon.

1870—Accepts position from United States Congress as head of a project to survey the region of the Rocky Mountains.

1871—Makes second trip down the Colorado River into the Grand Canyon; Emma Dean Powell gives birth to daughter, Mary.

1878—Publishes *Report on the Lands of the Arid Regions*, an important study outlining a plan for the careful development of the West that would preserve as much of the valuable land as possible.

1879—Becomes head of new Bureau of Ethnology.

1881—Replaces Clarence King as director of the United States Geological Survey; Continues as head of Bureau of Ethnology.

1894—Resigns from the Geological Survey.

1902—Dies in Haven, Maine.

CHAPTER NOTES

Chapter 1

1. John Wesley Powell, *The Exploration of the Colorado River and Its Canyons* (New York: Dover Publications, Inc., 1961), p. 247.

2. Merrill Beal, *Grand Canyon: The Story Behind the Scenery* (Las Vegas: KC Publications, Inc., 1983), p. 11.

3. Powell, p. 251.

Chapter 2

1. William Culp Darrah, *Powell of the Colorado* (Princeton, N.J.: Princeton University Press, 1951), pp. 4–5.

2. Robert Howard, "Powell of the Genessee," *The Westerners Brand Book, New York Posse*, 1969, pp. 26–28.

3. Howard, pp. 28–30; Darrah, pp. 11–15.

4. Darrah, p. 15.

5. Wallace Stegner, *Beyond the Hundredth Meridian: John Wesley Powell and the Second Opening of the West* (New York: Penguin Books, 1982), pp. 14–15; Patrick Washburn, "John Wesley Powell: Explorer of the Grand Canyon," *Boys' Life*, March 1994, p. 28.

6. Darrah, pp. 20–21.

7. Stegner, pp. 10–11; Darrah, pp. 24–25.

8. Darrah, pp. 34–35, 45.

9. Ibid., pp. 30–46.

10. Compiled Military Service Record of John Wesley Powell, National Archives, Washington, D.C. Powell enlisted at Cape Girardeau, Missouri, on October 8, 1861. He is listed as a captain in Battery F, 2nd Illinois Light Artillery.

Chapter 3

1. Compiled Military Service Record of John Wesley Powell, National Archives, Washington, D.C.

2. William Culp Darrah, *Powell of the Colorado* (Princeton, N.J.: Princeton University Press, 1951), pp. 58–59.

3. *Shiloh: National Military Park, Tennessee* (Washington, D.C.: National Park Service, U.S. Department of the Interior, 1996), p. 2.

4. John Y. Simon, ed., *The Papers of Ulysses S. Grant, Volume 5: April-August 31, 1862* (Carbondale, Ill: Southern Illinois University Press, 1973), p. 27.

5. Darrah, pp. 56–57.

6. Ibid., p. 59.

7. Ibid., p. 67.

8. Compiled Military Service Record of John Wesley Powell.

9. Wallace Stegner, *Beyond the Hundredth Meridian: John Wesley Powell and the Second Opening of the West* (New York: Penguin Books, 1982), p. 17.

10. Darrah, p. 65.

Chapter 4

1. Wallace Stegner, *Beyond the Hundredth Meridian: John Wesley Powell and the Second Opening of the West* (New York: Penguin Books, 1982), pp. 15–19.

2. William Culp Darrah, *Powell of the Colorado* (Princeton, N.J.: Princeton University Press, 1951), pp. 74–80.

3. John Wesley Powell, "Survey of the Colorado of the West," House of Representatives, 43rd Congress, 1st Session, Misc. Document No. 265, May 2, 1874, p. 6.

4. Darrah, pp. 81–89.

5. Bill Gilbert, *The Trailblazers* (New York: Time-Life Books, 1973), p. 102.

6. Stegner, pp. 18–21; Darrah, pp. 74–90.

Chapter 5

1. John Wesley Powell, *The Exploration of the Colorado River and Its Canyons* (New York: Dover Publications, Inc., 1961), pp. 35–37.

2. Joseph Judge, "Retracing John Wesley Powell's Historic Voyage Down the Grand Canyon," *National Geographic*, May 1969, p. 690.

3. Merrill Beal, *Grand Canyon: The Story Behind the Scenery* (Las Vegas: KC Publications, Inc., 1978) pp. 5–6, 36–37.

4. Quoted in Herman Viola, *Exploring the West* (Washington, D.C.: Smithsonian Books, 1987), p. 98.

5. Mary C. Rabbitt, *John Wesley Powell's Exploration of the Colorado River* (Washington, D.C.: U.S. Department of the Interior, 1978), p. 5; Bill Waters, "Lake Powell: A History-Rich Saga of High Adventure," *Arizona Highways*, April 1982, pp. 9–10.

6. William Culp Darrah, *Powell of the Colorado* (Princeton, N.J.: Princeton University Press, 1951), pp. 108–109.

7. Judge, p. 686.

8. William Goetzmann, "Explorer, Mountain Man, and Scientist," in *Exploring the American West, 1803–1879* (Washington, D.C.: Smithsonian Books, 1982), pp. 83–88; Viola, pp. 175–177.

9. Quoted in Rabbitt, p. 13.

10. Wallace Stegner, *Beyond the Hundredth Meridian: John Wesley Powell and the Second Opening of the West* (New York: Penguin Books, 1982), p. 64.

11. Powell, pp. 168–169.

12. Ibid.

13. Ibid., p. 191.

14. Ibid., p. 195.

15. Peter Miller, "John Wesley Powell: Vision for the West," *National Geographic*, April 1994, p. 103.

16. Stegner, pp. 77–107; Darrah, pp. 121–143.

Chapter 6

1. John Wesley Powell, *The Exploration of the Colorado River and Its Canyons* (New York: Dover Publications, Inc., 1961), p. 247.

2. Ibid., pp. 394–395.

3. Joseph Judge, "Retracing John Wesley Powell's Historic Voyage Down the Grand Canyon," *National Geographic*, May 1969, p. 698.

4. Powell, p. 256.

5. Ibid., p. 259.

6. Ibid., p. 264.

7. William Culp Darrah, *Powell of the Colorado* (Princeton, N.J.: Princeton University Press, 1951), pp. 140–141.

8. Ibid., p. 140.

9. Wallace Stegner, *Beyond the Hundredth Meridian: John Wesley Powell and the Second Opening of the West* (New York: Penguin Books, 1982), p. 107.

10. Judge, p. 710.

11. Mary Rabbitt, *John Wesley Powell's Exploration of the Colorado River* (Washington, D.C.: U.S. Department of the Interior, 1978), p. 76.

12. Powell, pp. 279–280.

13. Judge, p. 710.

14. Powell, p. 283.

15. Ibid., pp. 283–284.

16. Ibid., p. 285.

17. Stegner, pp. 110–111.

18. Darrah, p. 143.

19. Judge, p. 713.

20. Peter Miller, "John Wesley Powell: Vision for the West," *National Geographic*, April 1994, p. 103.

Chapter 7

1. Herman J. Viola, *Exploring the West* (Washington, D.C.: Smithsonian Books, 1987), p. 173.; U.S. Department of the Interior, *Exploring the American West, 1803–1879* (Washington, D.C.: United States National Park Service, 1982), pp. 83–89.

2. Viola, p. 174; *Exploring the American West*, pp. 91–92.

3. Viola, pp. 156–170.

4. Wallace Stegner, *Beyond the Hundredth Meridian: John Wesley Powell and the Second Opening of the West* (New York: Penguin Books, 1982), pp. 127–136; William Culp Darrah, *Powell of the Colorado* (Princeton, N.J.: Princeton University Press, 1951), pp. 144–159.

Chapter 8

1. William Culp Darrah, *Powell of the Colorado* (Princeton, N.J.: Princeton University Press, 1951), pp. 154–155.

2. Wallace Stegner, *Beyond the Hundredth Meridian: John Wesley Powell and the Second Opening of the West* (New York: Penguin Books, 1982), pp. 128–129.

3. Peter Miller, "John Wesley Powell: Vision for the West," *National Geographic*, April 1994, p. 104.

4. John Wesley Powell, *The Exploration of the Colorado River and Its Canyons* (New York: Dover Publications, Inc., 1961), p. 323.

5. Jacob Hamblin to Powell, December 20, 1870, Record Group 57, Records of the Geological Survey, Letters Received by John Wesley Powell, National Archives, Washington, D.C.

6. Darrah, p. 163.

7. Stegner, pp. 124–125.

8. Darrah, p. 168.

9. John Wesley Powell, "Survey of the Colorado of the West," House of Representatives, 43rd Congress, 1st Session, Misc. Document No. 265, May 2, 1874, p. 9.

10. Darrah, p. 176; Stegner, p. 137.

11. Stegner, pp. 140–142.

12. Ibid., p. 142.

13. Darrah, p. 191.

14. Ibid., p. 192.

15. "Frederick S. Dellenbaugh," *The New York Times*, January 31, 1935.

16. Darrah, p. 192.

17. Ibid.

18. Powell, *The Exploration of the Colorado River*, p. 394.

Chapter 9

1. William Culp Darrah, *Powell of the Colorado* (Princeton, N.J.: Princeton University Press, 1951), pp. 247, 386.

2. *Smithsonian Institution: 150:1846-1996* (Washington, D.C.: Smithsonian Institution, 1996), p. 1.

3. Ibid., p. 319.

4. John Wesley Powell, "Survey of the Colorado of the West," House of Representatives, 43rd Congress, 1st Session, Misc. Document No. 265, May 2, 1874, pp. 17–18.

5. Sandra D'Emilio and Suzan Campbell, *Visions and Visionaries: The Arts and Artists of the Santa Fe Railway* (Salt Lake City: Peregrine Smith, 1991), p. 9.

6. United States Department of the Interior, *Exploring the American West, 1803–1879* (Washington, D.C.: United States National Park Service, 1982), pp. 104–105.

7. Wallace Stegner, *Beyond the Hundredth Meridian: John Wesley Powell and the Second Opening of the West* (New York: Penguin Books, 1982), pp. 155–161.

8. Darrah, pp. 237–239.

Chapter 10

1. Alvin Josephy, *The Indian Heritage of America* (New York: Alfred Knopf, 1970), pp. 161–164, 333.

2. William Culp Darrah, *Powell of the Colorado* (Princeton, N.J.: Princeton University Press, 1951), p. 195.

3. Ibid., pp. 195–200.

4. Wallace Stegner, *Beyond the Hundredth Meridian: John Wesley Powell and the Second Opening of the West* (New York: Penguin Books, 1982), p. 181.

5. Darrah, p. 203.

6. Ibid., p. 204.

7. John Wesley Powell, "Are Our Indians Becoming Extinct?," *Forum*, May 1893, p. 353.

8. John Wesley Powell, "Survey of the Colorado of the West," House of Representatives, 43rd Congress, 1st Session, Misc. Document No. 265, May 2, 1874, p. 23.

9. Powell, "Are Our Indians Becoming Extinct?," pp. 346–354.

Chapter 11

1. John Wesley Powell, "The Irrigable Lands of the Arid Region," *Century Illustrated*, November 1889, pp. 766–770.

2. Ibid.

3. Winifred Blevins, *The Wordsworth Dictionary of the American West* (Hertfordshire, England: Wordsworth Editions, Ltd., 1993), p. 187.

4. William Culp Darrah, *Powell of the Colorado* (Princeton, N.J.: Princeton University Press, 1951), p. 224.

5. John Wesley Powell, *Report on the Lands of the Arid Region of the United States with a More Detailed Account of the Lands of Utah*, 45th Congress, 2nd Session, H.R. Exec. Doc. 73, Washington, D.C., 1878, p. 3.

6. Wallace Stegner, *Beyond the Hundredth Meridian: John Wesley Powell and the Second Opening of the West* (New York: Penguin Books, 1982), p. 239.

7. Everett Sterling, "The Powell Irrigation Survey, 1888–1893," *Mississippi Valley Historical Review*, December 1940, pp. 428–429.

8. Darrah, p. 254.

Chapter 12

1. Neil Judd, *The Bureau of American Ethnology* (Norman, Okla.: University of Oklahoma Press, 1967), pp. 1–4.

2. William Culp Darrah, *Powell of the Colorado* (Princeton, N.J.: Princeton University Press, 1951), p. 255.

3. Judd, p. 12.

4. Alvin Josephy, *The Indian Heritage of America* (New York: Alfred Knopf, 1970), p. 91.

5. Darrah, p. 296.

6. Wallace Stegner, *Beyond the Hundredth Meridian: John Wesley Powell and the Second Opening of the West* (New York: Penguin Books, 1982), p. 259.

7. Ibid., p. 241.

8. William Culp Darrah, *Powell of the Colorado* (Princeton, N.J.: Princeton University Press, 1951), pp. 245–247.

9. Ibid., pp. 243–251.

10. Quoted in Stegner, pp. 288–289.

11. Everett Sterling, "The Powell Irrigation Survey, 1888–1893," *Mississippi Valley Historical Review*, December 1940, p. 429.

12. Quoted in Stegner, p. 339.

13. Hamlin Garland, *A Son of the Middle Border* (New York: Macmillan Company, 1917), p. 308.

14. Quoted in Darrah, p. 304.

15. Sterling, pp. 427–433.

16. Quoted in Stegner, pp. 342–343.

Chapter 13

1. Henry Nash Smith, "Clarence King, John Wesley Powell, and the Establishment of the U.S. Geological Survey," *Mississippi Valley Historical Review*, June 1947, pp. 42–58.

2. Patrick Washburn, "John Wesley Powell: Explorer of the Grand Canyon," *Boys' Life*, March 1994, p. 28.

3. William Truettner, ed., *The West as America: Reinterpreting Images of the Frontier, 1820–1920* (Washington, D.C.: Smithsonian Institution Press, 1991), p. 21; John Wesley Powell, "The Irrigable Lands of the Arid Region," *Century Illustrated*, November 1889, p. 769.

4. Peter Miller, "John Wesley Powell: Vision for the West," *National Geographic*, April 1994, p. 114.

5. Everett Sterling, "The Powell Irrigation Survey, 1888–1893," *Mississippi Valley Historical Review*, December 1940, p. 434.

6. Wallace Stegner, *Beyond the Hundredth Meridian: John Wesley Powell and the Second Opening of the West* (New York: Penguin Books, 1982), p. 355.

7. William Culp Darrah, *Powell of the Colorado* (Princeton, N.J.: Princeton University Press, 1951), p. 332.

8. Ibid.

9. Stegner, p. xxii.

10. Ibid.

11. Darrah, p. 391.

12. Quoted in Miller, p. 114.

13. Darrah, pp. 324–325.

GLOSSARY

archaeology—The scientific study of the life and culture of ancient peoples.

artillery—The branch of the Army specializing in the use of heavy mounted guns.

Confederacy—Southern states that seceded from the United States between 1860 and 1861.

conservation—Care and protection of the earth's natural resources from loss and waste.

dam—Barrier built to hold back or divert flowing water.

Death Valley—Dry, hot desert area in Eastern California and Southern Nevada in which is located the lowest point in the Western Hemisphere—282 feet below sea level.

entomology—The study of insects.

ethnology—The study of the historical development and characteristics of the races and cultures of mankind.

fossil—Hardened remains of plant or animal life preserved in rock.

geology—Science dealing with the physical nature and history of the earth.

homestead—Tract of public land granted by the United States government for development to a settler.

irrigation—Supplying the land with water by means of artificial ditches, channels, dams, and other means.

kiva—Sacred underground room used by ancient Native Americans for religious services.

Mormon—Member of the Church of Jesus Christ of Latter-day Saints. The church was founded in the United States in 1830.

natural history—Study of geology, mineralogy, and other subjects dealing with the physical world.

Pike's Peak—Mountain peak in Colorado named after the famous American explorer, Zebulon Pike, who attempted unsuccessfully to reach its summit in 1806.

reservation—Public land set aside by the United States government for use by Native American populations.

reservoir—Natural or artificial lake or pond in which water is collected and stored for use.

rooster tails—Places in rapidly flowing streams and rivers where the water explodes against rocks below the surface and rises into view.

Smithsonian Institution—Institution and museum founded in 1846 in Washington, D.C., through a gift from an English scientist named James Smithson. The branches of the Smithsonian include a wide range of fields in the arts and sciences.

Union—A term used to describe the nation of the United States of America, especially during the Civil War.

whirlpool—Water in rapid, violent, whirling motion tending to form a circle into which floating objects are drawn.

FURTHER READING

Darrah, William Culp. *Powell of the Colorado.* Princeton, NJ: Princeton University Press, 1951.

D'Emilio, Sandra, and Suzan Campbell. *Visions and Visionaries: The Art and Artists of the Santa Fe Railway.* Salt Lake City: Peregrine Smith, 1991.

Garland, Hamlin. *A Son of the Middle Border.* New York: Macmillan Company, 1917.

Hobbs, William H. "John Wesley Powell, 1834–1902." *Scientific Monthly*, December 1934, pp. 519–524.

Howard, Robert. "Powell of the Genessee." *The Westerners Brand Book, New York Posse*, 1969, pp. 25–32.

Josephy, Alvin M. *The Indian Heritage of America.* New York: Alfred Knopf, 1970.

Judd, Neil. *The Bureau of American Ethnology.* Norman, OK: University of Oklahoma Press, 1967.

Judge, Joseph. "Retracing John Wesley Powell's Historic Voyage Down the Grand Canyon." *National Geographic*, May 1969, pp. 668–713.

Miller, Peter. "John Wesley Powell: Vision for the West." *National Geographic*, April 1994, pp. 93–114.

National Archives and Records Administration, Washington, DC, Compiled Military Service Record of John Wesley Powell.

National Archives and Records Administration, Washington, DC, Record Group 57, Records of the U.S. Geological Survey, Letters Received by John Wesley Powell, Director of the Geographical and Geological Survey of the Rocky Mountain Region, 1869–79 (Available in National Archives Microcopy Number 156).

Powell, John Wesley. "Are Our Indians Becoming Extinct?" *Forum*, May 1893, pp. 343–354.

———. *Report on the Lands of the Arid Regions of the United States with a More Detailed Account of the Lands of Utah*, 45th Congress, 2nd Session, H.R. Exec. Doc. 73. Washington, DC: 1878.

———."Survey of the Colorado of the West." House of Representatives, 43rd Congress, 1st Session, Misc. Document No. 265, May 2, 1874.

———. *The Exploration of the Colorado River and Its Canyons*. New York: Dover Publications, Inc., 1961.

———. "The Irrigable Lands of the Arid Region." *Century Illustrated*, November 1889, pp. 766–770.

Rabbitt, Mary. *John Wesley Powell's Exploration of the Colorado River*. Washington, DC: Department of the Interior, 1978.

Shiloh: National Military Park, Tennessee. Washington, DC: National Park Service, U.S. Department of the Interior, 1996.

Smith, Henry Nash. "Clarence King, John Wesley Powell, and the Establishment of the U.S. Geological Survey." *Mississippi Valley Historical Review*, June 1947, pp. 36–57.

Stegner, Wallace. *Beyond the Hundredth Meridian: John Wesley Powell and the Second Opening of the West*. New York: Penguin Books, 1982.

Sterling, Everett. "The Powell Irrigation Survey, 1888–1893," *Mississippi Valley Historical Review*, December 1940, pp. 421–434.

Truettner, William, ed. *The West as America: Reinterpreting Images of the Frontier, 1820–1920*. Washington, DC: Smithsonian Institution Press, 1991.

United States Department of the Interior. *Exploring the American West, 1803–1879*. Washington, DC: United States National Park Service, 1982.

Viola, Herman. *Exploring the West*. Washington, DC: Smithsonian Books, 1987.

Walker, Stephen. *Arizona: The Grand Canyon State*. Flagstaff, AZ: Canyonlands Publications, 1991.

Washburn, Patrick. "John Wesley Powell: Explorer of the Grand Canyon." *Boys' Life*, March 1994.

Waters, Bill. "Lake Powell: A History-Rich Saga of High Adventure." *Arizona Highways*, April 1982, pp. 6–13.

INDEX